Rave Reviews

Stacey doesn't know just how gifted she is. The magic she creates is about much more than 'her story.' As compelling as her life lessons are, what's equally as profound is how Stacey has seen through those challenges. She sees her life through the filter of many potent gifts. There's phenomenal wisdom in that yet it's unconscious for her. Spend time with Stacey and you'll feel her pure state of non-judgment. The degree to which it's true can only come from someone with the gift of deep empathy.
Shaune Clarke—

The rich get richer, the poor can too!

If you are powered by passion... ...all things are possible

Stacey Currie

Balboa Press books may be ordered through booksellers or by contacting:

Balboa Press
A Division of Hay House
1663 Liberty Drive
Bloomington, IN 47403
www.balboapress.com
1-(877) 407-4847

ISBN: 978-1-4525-0291-5 (sc)
ISBN: 978-1-4525-0292-2 (ebk)

Printed in the United States of America

Balboa Press rev. date: 04/24/2012

Acknowledgements

I know I could never have achieved all that I have without the support of those close to me.

Dave

Davey my baby what a pleasure to have met you. If there is one man on this planet who could tolerate me and my ambitious nature, it is you. We are like chalk and cheese however we share so many traits: the love of our children, our determination, motivation, vision and ambition, not to mention the fact we love to give each other space and support each other's desire to have our own hobbies.

I love how you have nurtured my softer, loving Mum side, the side no one ever got to see, the side I never got to express. I love how you don't control me, you support my purpose and you understand my independent ways.

I used to dream and visualise about having a partner like you, living in our dream house with our happy family. I can't believe I am now living that dream. I know I can be a challenge at times but I love the way you 'get' me.

I am truly thankful that I gave in and accepted the invitation to watch you go-kart. I can't begin to imagine where my life could have led to without you in it. Not only did you take on my children, but you also took on me and my baggage. You have been so patient, knowing that everything will fall into place, knowing that with love and support surrounding them, my children would come out on top and knowing that through nurturing my strengths I could realise my goals and live my dreams.

You are the best partner I could have asked for. Actually you are better than the one I used to dream about. In my dreams we had a few arguments; I can't believe we don't fight. You are an amazing Dad to our babies and they are so lucky to have you. I love you so much and can't wait to get married and live happily ever after. I'm still in shock that you asked me to marry you.

My Children

Thankyou to my five beautiful children. You have each been such a gift – individual and special in your own ways. I have learnt so much from you that has made me the person I am today.

I am so proud of you all and can't wait to see where your journey takes you.

Dad, Dave and the kids, I thank you from the bottom of my heart and love you all so much.

Preface

Every year when the government budget was announced I would hear the same thing. 'It's all for the rich. The rich get richer, the poor get poorer'. I didn't want to believe this was true. Weren't some of the rich people poor people once? Wasn't it possible that they had worked hard to become rich? I responded 'Yes, the rich get richer, but the poor can too'. I wanted to show people that it was possible for the poor to become rich. I told myself that one day I would write a book called 'The Rich Get Richer, The Poor Can Too'. And when I say I'll do something, I do it.

I stumbled through life and had to scramble over many obstacles to find the answers I needed. I moved past having no Mum, being sexually abused at the age of nine, falling pregnant at the age of fifteen, being homeless with two babies, living in a violent relationship with three children at twenty one, to now living a life filled with all my dreams and goals. I have five wonderful children and a beautiful and supportive partner. We live in my dream home by the beach and run a successful business for which I was nominated in the 2010 Telstra Business Women's Awards. The most exciting part of my life right now is being an Ambassador for the Lighthouse Foundation's Mums 'n Bubs homes. I did become rich: rich in family, rich in wealth, rich in health, rich in love, rich in my whole life.

Luckily for me I had a clear vision and a passion to keep me going. It's amazing what you can achieve when you have a passion. If I had not had my passion and the self belief to make it happen, I don't know if I would have made it. I truly believe that 'If you are powered by passion, all things are possible'.

It took me years to find the right direction…, the right solutions…, the right way for myself and my children. When I finally discovered that my visions and actions could actually transform my life into the life I had dreamt of, I threw myself in boots and all. Then I was inspired to empower as many women as possible to discover their own passions and dreams and make them a reality too.

Not only am I fulfilling my own dream but I hope to help you fulfil YOUR dreams too.

Go on; make today the new beginning of your new successful life…

Contents

PART ONE
Stacey's Story

PART TWO
Action Steps

PART THREE
Where to Next

Part One

STACEY'S STORY

How My Dream Began

My dream started when I was twenty one years old and living in a violent relationship. I was lost. I had no real friends, I was angry, I was lonely and my children were suffering. My self esteem was gone and I had really hit the bottom of the black hole. I also had three children aged five, two, and four months old to care for.

One night after yet another violent argument with my partner, I found myself at the Royal Children's Hospital. My son had been admitted after being physically hurt. It was 2am and there I was, crammed into a little room with my three children, officers from the Department of Human Services, some Federal Police and a few staff from the hospital.

They questioned me for a very long time about the relationship I was living in, and how my son was hurt. I was grilled about why I was staying in this abusive relationship and why I was putting my children through it all.

After a couple of hours of this I was asked to leave the room. I sat out in the waiting room until eventually they called me back in. I was told that I had to get myself and my children out of the situation I was in. All the authorities who were represented in that room had discussed my situation and as of today I had two choices.

My first choice was that I could stay in the relationship and have my three children placed into foster care. I remember dropping to my knees begging them not to take my children from me. Then they offered the second choice.

If I took the second choice I could keep my children but I must change my life. The conditions were that, beginning immediately, I would be court ordered to not have anything to do with my violent partner for twelve weeks. In those twelve weeks, I would have to attend a domestic violence counsellor. I wanted desperately to keep my children but couldn't see how I could possibly change my life.

That night I was forced to make the best choice of my whole life. That night the dream began.

I went along to the domestic violence group, thinking that I really did not belong as I was not bruised and battered. As it was court ordered though, I had to attend. For some reason I remember exactly what I was wearing the first time I went along – a little pair of blue denim shorts and a red singlet top. I was trying to hide my legs because I felt so fat and disgusting. I was a size eight. I remember telling my counsellor Donna that I felt very ugly.

Although I started with a negative attitude, after a while I started to realise that the group was really helping to build up my self esteem. The sessions were every Tuesday and Saturday and I attended them without fail. They even had a childcare facility where my children could be safely minded. The Tuesday sessions always finished at 3pm and I would head straight to the school afterwards to pick up Josh. Every Tuesday after the session I would stride into school as confident as the Queen. I was on cloud nine, so excited about what was happening.

However even with all the help of the group, it was extremely hard for me to just walk away from my partner. I really thought I loved him. One day I was feeling really depressed and was sorely tempted to slip back into the relationship. I knew that if I was caught I would lose my children and felt like I must be the worst Mum alive. I asked for guidance from my counsellor Donna. She said 'Stacey, go and hire a book from the library'. I looked at her blankly and replied 'Is that all you can recommend? I really hate books'.

By that point I had gained a tremendous amount of respect for Donna. I was finding that everything she told me was true, so I had a lot of trust in her. After that session I went to my local library and hired a book on sexual abuse. It was BRILLIANT! For the past two years I had been told every day that I was a psycho, insecure, a scum bag, a slut. Now, for the first time in my life I started to feel normal. All the emotions I was experiencing were totally normal. My favourite part of the book was the exercises to help turn all that negativity around, get over my issues and create a successful life for myself and my children. I took action on all the learnings and watched in amazement as my life soon started to transform. My self esteem reached an all time high. I felt great, I truly loved who I was becoming and felt like the best Mum to my children. I even felt attractive for the first time in my life.

After this I became addicted to reading and self development. In the ten years since then, I have read a book every week. The topics vary depending on the issues I am facing at the time. I have read books on self esteem, parenting and anger. I have read business books, books on marketing, I have read the stories of entrepreneurs, successful women, successful business owners and many many more.

As I read, I started to realise that all successful people have some things in common. We all read books, we all have a strong commitment, we are all motivated, we all face our fears and we all have strong values.

I remember reading one day on the internet about a woman who was only thirty years old and had built a very successful business. I read everything I could about this lady; how she began, the obstacles and hurdles she had faced, everything I could find. I'd had a dream since I was eight years old of owning my own business. After reading this lady's story, I knew I could make my dream a reality.

I wanted to know more about successful women. Why were they so confident and successful when I wasn't? What was their secret? I wanted to be able to network with them without feeling intimidated or thinking they were better than me. I became obsessed with learning everything I could about successful women. With each learning, I realised more and more that I was just as good as these women, even though they were all older than me. I could become just as successful as they were if I wanted to. I had no more excuses. It was up to me.

My next goal was to surround myself with friends who had a positive outlook. I started to look for positive young Mums. I attended a young Mums' group but it just was not for me. They spent their time talking about drinking, partying, smoking; all the things I did not want to be involved in. I struggled to find the people I wanted to be around, so I googled successful young Mums and positive young Mums. I looked at the library for books on young Mums. I could not believe that there was nothing positive to be found relating to young Mums.

By now I had become involved in our current business, Signs 'n' Banners, so I started to attend business women's functions. I found I was extremely intimidated by the older women there. It had nothing to do with the women themselves; it was my own lack of self esteem getting in the way. I had come so far, and yet I could see that my self esteem still had a long way to go.

Then something amazing happened. Successful women who were older than me started to call asking for my advice. Women running million dollar companies were calling me! We talked about everything from managing a work/life balance to business marketing and beyond. It finally occurred to me that I had become the business woman I dreamt of being. I got over my feelings of intimidation and actually started enjoying being around these women. I no longer felt different to them, in fact some of them were actually inspired by me. What an eye opener.

With all this great feedback I was feeling on top of the world. I decided it was time that other young Mums had someone who cared about them, to teach them what I had learned. Then they too could experience a happy, colourful, successful life.

I created www.EmpoweringYoungMums.com.au and started running workshops with young Mums. The workshops were free, as I was simply sharing my passion. I couldn't believe it when journalists began to call, asking me to do stories for their magazines, newspapers and TV shows. I was simply sharing what was in my heart and people wanted to interview me about it.

I began to realise that I could help transform so many more women's lives by empowering them to take action. I knew the time had come to get this information out to young Mums everywhere, so I started writing.

I wrote my story from the beginning; my early days as a child, having my babies so young, having nowhere to live, being in a violent relationship. Then I wrote how I turned it around and I kept on writing, describing how I live now. My incredible new life, full of laughter, happiness, noise and peace. A life where I am making my dreams happen and most importantly, a life where my children and I are happy.

Soon some themes emerged, topics based around how I overcame obstacles to be the successful woman I am today. Now I can share my learnings with you and others in the hope you will find some ideas to help you take action just as I did and transform your life into the life of your dreams.

Childhood

I am so grateful that my childhood was not violent. Chaotic yes, but not violent. I do remember wishing I had a Mum though. I don't have any memories of living with my Mum, I was so young when my parents split up and I went to live with Dad.

Growing up in a housing commission area we were surrounded by poor families. We were just another of the poor families in our neighbourhood. However we were one of those families people tell their kids not to hang out with because we were 'trouble'. My Dad and stepmum were not alcoholics, drug addicts or gamblers; they just had no idea how to bring up kids. We had absolutely no discipline whatsoever, which had its down side but could also be a lot of fun.

As a seven year old I was often left at home to look after my newborn brother Michael. One particular day I had been alone for hours with the screaming baby. I had tried to change his nappy and accidentally pricked his penis with the nappy pin. Eventually I realised I couldn't manage the nappy on my own and ran next door with him to ask our neighbours to help me. Once this was done I raced back home as I was also looking after my two year old sister. As they were both crying, I decided to take them for a walk. I put them both in the pram and off we went. As a seven year old I thought it would be pretty cool to make it more exciting and so I ran, jumping over hills and bumps with the pram. Of course it never occurred to me to strap the babies into the pram. After going over a great hill, the pram flew forward with a jolt. My sister hit the pavement and cut her lip, while the newborn baby tumbled out onto the path without being hurt. I scrambled to put them both back into the pram and get home to fix my sister's lip, terrified of getting into trouble. Most people wouldn't leave a seven year old in charge of such small children, but this was our family and that was the way we were.

I will always remember how much my Dad loved my brothers, sisters and I, and all the great times we had. Life was not all gloom and doom. We lived close to the beach and Dad would take us there most days after school and on weekends. We would have the whole neighbourhood crowded into our van for a trip to the beach.

Sometimes we would jump into the van and go to the bush with other families to play hide and seek in our cars. We would cover the cars with bushes and the other family had to find us. Then we would swap and the other family would hide and we had to find them. Dad would even use his van to go four wheel driving. Dad was just like a great big kid, I can't even begin to explain how fun it was to be bought up by him. I am just thankful I survived.

At one point my stepmum was in hospital for around nine months, after complications with a hysterectomy. Dad was working fulltime and so during the school holidays my three brothers, my sister and myself, all under the age of ten, were at home alone. We were really bored on this particular day and thought it would be a great idea to knock down the lounge room wall. We phoned Dad at work and asked if we could knock down the wall. Dad was thinking we would be knocking down a garden wall out in the backyard so he agreed. When he arrived home he got the shock of his life – the whole lounge room wall had been knocked down. We still crack up laughing at that to this day.

Another vivid memory is the waterbed incident. We kids were always looking for an adventure, so we decided to inflate an old waterbed mattress with the vacuum cleaner and bounce each other. One person would sit on the end of the mattress while the other person ran and jumped on the other end, bouncing the person sitting on it into the air. We were having a great time when Dad came home from work. Well Dad was a big man and a kid himself, so he wanted to play. Being the tomboy, I jumped at the chance to sit on the end and have him bounce me. I was waiting all excited and then 'whoosh' I went flying up into the air. I went past the house roof and then came back down and landed on the ground, right on my arm. I was screaming in agony and Dad kept saying 'Shut up, the neighbours will hear'. He was too embarrassed to try to explain to them what had happened. Eventually we went to the hospital to have my broken arm set. This would be one of six broken arms I have had through my life.

We had some great times around the house. Out the back was a huge tree which we would use as our cubby house. The tree was at least twenty feet tall and we had climbed right to the top and nailed boards to each branch to make seats for each of us. We would play in that tree for hours. We even had a rope with a crate attached to it that would bring our dinner up, so we could sit in the top of the tree to eat our meal.

One very windy day we had a friend over to play. We had found a large outdoor umbrella on the side of the road and took it home, knowing we could make some use of it. We were up in the tree house when a great idea popped into one of our heads. I yelled out to my brothers to bring up the umbrella so we could fly out of the tree like Mary Poppins. I was first to go and used the umbrella to parachute neatly to the ground. Then it was our friend's turn, however he was very underweight. As he jumped with the umbrella, the wind caught him and off he went, sailing right over the fence and eventually landing in our neighbour's yard. We were all laughing so hard we could not even go and help the poor scared kid. He came from a very strict family and he could never imagine doing something like this. Luckily his parents never found out. Now I understand why we always had the neighbourhood kids sneaking over to play at our house – we always had so much fun. With no parents watching, we could do whatever we wanted.

Dad worked for a water purification company and would bring home large empty barrels. Being the adventurous kids we were, we knew we could come up with a great idea. 'Hey guys, why don't we put each other in the barrel and roll it around the yard?' I yelled. We were all excited by our new game and took it in turns in rolling each other around with the lid off. You know how it is, you do something for a while and it all seems fun. Then after you have done it for an hour, you want to go to the next level. Well I was ready for the next level. We told our brother to get into the barrel with the lid on this time, to go down the stairs. In he jumped and we tightened up the lid. That barrel rolled down the stairs and then kept going all the way down our street. As the barrel finally rolled to a stop in the middle of the road, the poor kid got out looking like he had seen a ghost. We were crying with laughter and couldn't wait to all have a turn.

Dad always made sure Christmas was amazing for us. I think he would use three months worth of wages to fund Christmas, and we would regularly be in arrears with the rent around that time of year. On Christmas night we kids would all sleep together in one room. We were so excited no one got much sleep though. Dad would wake us up about 4.30am to tell us Santa had been. Into the lounge room we would go to find hundreds of presents. When I say hundreds it was no exaggeration. By about 5.30am we would all be out in the street playing with our new toys. Dad was just a great big kid who allowed us to have so much fun.

My childhood taught me that just because you are a parent does not mean you can't have fun with your children. I was always encouraged to try new things, and have bought this into my own parenting. I have also learnt however that parenting can't be all fun. Children need boundaries, rules and discipline. Because I hadn't experienced these myself I struggled to understand how soft or strict these rules and boundaries should be.

I once rode my son's Pee Wee 80 motorbike to a birthday party to pick him up, thinking it would be a great surprise. I couldn't comprehend why everyone was so shocked when I arrived. It didn't occur to me that it was illegal and dangerous to ride this tiny bike on the road, let alone with no helmet.

Another time I bought a swimming pool that was almost the same size as our courtyard garden. We could only just squeeze it in next to the trampoline. We thought it was just great – we could either jump from the trampoline into the pool or off the house roof into the pool!

Slowly I learned the difference between having fun and putting us all in danger. I began to listen to my intuition and find boundaries that worked for my family. We still have a lot of fun but I am enjoying having a better balance.

The Little Runt

My nickname when I was a young girl was 'runt'. I thought it was funny and loved to have people call me by my nickname. Now of course I understand the meaning of a runt. I guess even as a child people picked up on how different I was.

I look back at my school photos and see the stained, dirty clothes I would arrive at school in. It takes me back to memories of my adventures on the way to school. Dad was always working and I didn't get along with my stepmum so I would get up extra early, get myself ready and then rain, hail or shine would head off for the ten kilometre walk to school.

Sometimes I would walk with my brothers, sometimes alone. I didn't like to be at home when Dad wasn't there, so I would often leave home at 6am and not return home until 11pm at night. Because we lived in a street where there were a few families like ours, we would all get together and play tiggy until late at night. Even on the weekends I would be out all day, having adventures.

Someone told me that there were wild pigs living in the creek so I explored around the creek before school, trying to spot one. By the time I arrived at school I was covered from head to toe in dirt. I must have had one of those adventures on school photo day – I was filthy! I never did see those pigs; I think someone was pulling my leg.

This didn't help my reputation too much; I was frequently teased for being unclean. I had a lot of friends but even they teased me for having dirty clothes and a dirty house.

I rarely bought my friends home to play as I was so embarrassed about the state of our house. One day I invited one of my best friends for a sleep over. The house looked like a tornado had been through it as usual.

Our laundry was off the back verandah and was the size of a bedroom. The laundry floor was always waist deep in dirty clothes which we would wade through if we were looking for something. Sometimes the clothes sat for so long on the floor they would go mouldy. I remember our neighbour quite regularly coming over to do our washing. My bedroom walls also suffered from mould; there was not a dry patch to be seen. I didn't have a wardrobe so kept my clothes in a big grey steel industrial filing cabinet.

After the sleepover, my friend went back to school and told everyone about my mouldy room, dirty laundry and the kitchen where dirty dishes were piled almost to the roof.

After this I became obsessed with cleaning, and would scrub my bedroom every weekend – walls, furniture, windows, everything. I tried bleach but it didn't work, so I had a go with foaming tyre cleaner. I sprayed the whole room with the foam and scrubbed like crazy but the mould always came back.

Sometimes I would share my room with various brothers and sisters. At one point there were five of us sharing a bedroom, once I shared with my sister, and once I even had my own room. If I was sharing a room I would draw a line on the floor to show where my section was. No-one was allowed to touch my area and I always kept it nice and clean.

Through all of this I began to understand the effect your personal appearance and that of your environment can have on your self esteem. I have learnt to take pride in my appearance and my home and enjoy the extra confidence this brings.

Assaulted

When I was nine years old Mum offered for my brother and me to stay at her house. I was so excited to finally be staying at Mum's as I hadn't seen her in a long time. Late in the evening Mum had to go to the local pub where she worked, so she left us at home with a male friend, as it was bedtime anyway.

The man had put the other kids to bed and made a bed for me on the lounge. The memories of that night are still so vivid, even down to the itchy material covering the lounge. I fell asleep next to the man, who was watching television and drinking beer. Suddenly I woke, feeling his hand lift my nighty and pull my undies down. I was sexually abused that night.

A few times the man got up and went into the kitchen. I could hear the fridge open so I can only guess he was getting another beer. Each time he would walk out of the room I would pull my undies up and pull my nighty down then turn over, clasping my legs tightly together. Whenever he came back in I pretended to be asleep, trying not to breathe too loudly in the hope he wouldn't want to wake me up. I was frozen to the spot with fear.

When I woke up in the morning I just wanted to go home. For many years I didn't tell anyone what happened to me, but it was the last time I ever slept at that house. If I was supposed to stay there I would scream and grab hold of Dad's leg. No one could understand why and no one ever asked. Dad just assumed I did not like my Mum, which wasn't the case at all.

Eventually Mum moved house. Mum's new house seemed different. I felt safe and so decided to stay over. This time when she went to work she arranged for my cousin to babysit us. We were all playing around, laughing and joking. I don't exactly remember how it came out but I told my cousin what had happened to me, just laughing about it. As my cousin was a lot older than me, she took it quite seriously and phoned my Mum at work to tell her what I had said. Mum came home and asked me about it. I remember feeling so scared, thinking I was going to get into big trouble. I started making excuses, saying that the man was drinking a lot of beer and maybe he did not remember it, trying to get myself out of the situation.

Mum then asked Dad and my stepmum to come over to her unit, saying she wanted to talk to them about something. The kids were told to go into the bedroom while the adults had a talk. On the way home in the car, I heard Dad saying to my stepmum that Mum was making this up and it was just a trick to win her upcoming court battle. After that it was many years before I would talk to anyone again about what had happened to me. I felt that if my Dad, the man I loved more than anyone else, did not believe me, then who would?

For the rest of that year, I seemed to be in trouble every single day at school. I was in grade four and I believe the assault affected the rest of my primary school years. I was known as the naughty girl in the school. It didn't bother me to swear at my teachers; I knew I would not get into trouble at home so why should I be scared?

Like many schools, we had a corridor off the class room where the naughty children would sit. This would become my most regular seat, as I was kicked out of the classroom every day for misbehaving and disrupting the class. In the end the Principal was concerned I would get piles from the cold floor so they organised a chair just for me to sit on.

Nevertheless I got along with all my teachers and was a caring friend at school. I just found it really difficult to concentrate, and was doing all I could to get attention. I guess it was my way of crying out for help.

One of my teachers must have known something was not right, as she spent a lot of time talking with me and trying to help me. I was in this particular teacher's class when there was a knock at the door.

In walked a man with glasses, asking to see me in his room. I froze and said 'No I am not going'. My teacher was trying to force me so I crawled under her table and held on to the leg of the table for dear life. I had no trust in any man; I was absolutely petrified of being in a room alone with him. Eventually I ended up going to his office, where he asked me to draw pictures of certain things and talked to me about my home life. Now I understand that the school was trying to find out what was happening to me so they could help me. However my own Dad had not believed me when he found out what happened, so why should I tell this stranger?

The big camp of the year was coming up and all the grade fours were going to Canberra. I was so excited about camp, however I had conditions for attendance set by my teachers and Principal. I had to behave until camp day. This was a tough condition for me as I was in trouble every single day. I decided to give it my best shot as I really wanted to go to camp. We had about two weeks to go until camp and I was nearly there, achieving the results my teachers were looking for. I had been on my best behaviour for the last few months. One day my brother came running into my classroom asking for me. We went into the corridor where he told me his teacher had hit him with a ruler. I was extremely protective of all of my brothers and sisters, so I went straight to his teacher and confronted him about why he hit my brother. All my anger from the past few months came out and boy did I let loose.

At assembly the following day, the Principal asked all the grade four students to stand up. He announced that everyone standing would be off to Canberra in a couple of week's time, with the exception of one student. I was so humiliated. I felt like such a failure after trying so hard to behave. I had been so proud of my behaviour in the last couple of months; my teachers had even rewarded me with a Mars Bar. At home that night I cried and cried. 'Why can't I be good?' I thought, 'Why am I so naughty?' I just could not understand why I was not normal. I did go to a camp in the end – I was sent for three weeks to a camp in Sydney for underprivileged and troubled children.

Around this time I became extremely scared of the dark and would bribe my brothers and sisters to sleep in my bedroom with me. After a while they didn't want to sleep with me any more, and I could focus on nothing else. I would spend every day at school anxiously trying to come up with new bribes. I did manage to convince them to stay each and every night; had I not had them around that time I have no idea what I would have done.

My anxiety got to the point where I would scream and cry when Dad would leave for work, as I was scared to stay at home alone. Dad drove taxis and I begged him to take me with him. We were very close and he would do anything I wanted. One night Dad took me with him after one of my tantrums. Dad and I went to the train station in his taxi to pick up a customer, however when we arrived there were actually four men waiting for the taxi. As there was no room for me in the car, I had to wait alone at the train station at 11.00pm at night until Dad came back. I waited there curled up in a ball under a street light crying my eyes out, shaking with fear.

As I grew older I wanted some closure about what had happened to me as a child. I had learnt that what happened was not my fault, and that I was not a bad person because this had happened to me. I was able to talk with my own children about sexual assault and help them understand how important it is to speak up if they are uncomfortable with someone's actions.

I didn't want to carry this pain with me for the rest of my life and allow it to keep hurting me. So when I was twenty one and pregnant with my third baby, I took the matter to court. Although the perpetrator was found not guilty, at least he was forced to face what he had done.

I refused to allow what had happened to be an excuse for me not to achieve what I wanted with my life. I was able to leave it behind and move on with my life.

Girl on a Mission

Growing up in a poor family taught me to work hard. If I wanted something, I had to make it happen myself.

At fourteen, my boyfriend and I were living in a shed in the back yard of Dad's house in Melbourne. He was the same age as me and would become the father of my first two children. If we were cold we would get all the rubbish out of our bin and start a fire inside the shed to warm up. My lifestyle was not the best but I was happy as I had no rules or boundaries. I was free to be me and live the life I wanted.

My boyfriend and I were like best friends, hanging out together and climbing trees. I felt truly attached to someone for the first time in my life. He came from a very good family and was doing really well at school as well as being a promising tae-kwon-do student. He had a great future ahead of him, and as I look back now I can understand the devastation his parents felt when he met me. He moved out of his beautiful family home to live with me in my shed where we could do whatever we liked. He started wagging school, quit playing sport and basically became nothing while we were together. I am so pleased that he has also transformed his life and is now happily married and has gone on to become very successful.

I loved visiting his house though and often asked him if we could stay with them. It was clean and comfortable at their house and I just loved being around positive, driven people. Of course he loved my house where there were no rules and he could do what he liked. He lived with us for many years.

Like most fourteen year olds, at this age I started to take more notice of how I looked. Although I preferred boys' clothes, I couldn't help but notice that many of my friends were wearing really nice top brand clothes and I wasn't. My boyfriend and some of my other friends came from well-to-do families and they all seemed to wear great looking top brand clothes. The in thing to wear at the time was a Country Road jumper and Cross Colour jeans. I desperately wanted to buy my boyfriend a Country Road jumper and myself a pair of Cross Colour jeans.

One day we were at my boyfriend's parents' house. His mum was showing him how to look for a job, and had the local paper out on the bench. As she circled jobs he could apply for with her pen, she said that all he needed to do was to call and ask for an interview. I thought 'Hey, how easy is that?'. I went home, got the Yellow Pages out and rang all the local businesses to ask for a job. I felt like the luckiest person on the planet when I was offered a job in a local factory, putting their Easter Egg hampers together. I worked on a Saturday and was paid $70 for the day. I was so excited that I did buy that jumper for my boyfriend. After that I continued to give him my wages every Saturday. I had never had money before and was happy to just give it away and help others. I suppose watching my Dad constantly help people taught me to do the same.

Eventually I quit the factory job as I wanted to work somewhere better. I thought I would move up in the world so I walked in to the local newsagency and asked for a job there. I felt on top of the world when I got that job. Every day after school my boyfriend would give me a ride to work on a bike we had found on the hard rubbish.

From then on I became quite entrepreneurial and knew how to turn a profit. Dad used to babysit kids on the weekend. My sister would also have her friends staying over and most of the time we were left alone in the house while Dad went out. As I was making money from my newsagency job, I decided to get Chinese food for lunch one Saturday. Of course the other four kids who were at our house wanted some also. Chinese lunch meals were $8.00 each and I didn't have enough money for everyone, so I got the kids together and said 'Guys, let's go and make some money for lunch'.

I knocked on the door of all the houses in our street and asked them if they needed any cleaning done. Once I'd won a sale, I got the kids to clean the house. Then I would go back, collect the money, gather the kids and we would all walk to the Chinese restaurant and order lunch. This became a regular money-making adventure each Saturday.

Not all my money-making schemes were such a good idea. I went through a phase of shoplifting then selling the proceeds. I would steal cigarettes and then sell them at school, and when the Batman Movie came out all the girls loved the false fingernails I was stealing for them. With the money I made I took Dad and my stepmum out for dinner and they got food poisoning from the lobster. It must have been karma! Eventually I was caught stealing clothes and was so humilated that I never shoplifted again.

As time went on, I left the newsagency and began working every day after school as a waitress in a cafe. My determination to succeed showed in my work – I was a great employee, always on time, never afraid to work hard and quick to learn so that I could get ahead.

I had learnt from a young age that if I wanted something I didn't have, I was the only one stopping me from having it. I didn't dwell on what I didn't have. Coming from a poor family helped me develop a lot of skills in self sufficiency and I actually enjoyed the challenge of making things happen for myself.

Fifteen, Pregnant and No Idea

Growing up without my Mum was difficult in many ways. I missed out on all those mother-daughter chats, even the one about the birds and the bees. I wasn't aware of the consequences of having sex and I didn't know the symptoms of pregnancy. I had no idea I was pregnant for quite a while.

Dad was standing in the kitchen showing me the hernia on his great big belly. I could see a sizeable lump and said 'Yeah, I have one of those on my belly too Dad'. Dad thought I had better get it checked out, so as I was a very independent girl I took myself off to the doctors to ask them to help me with my hernia. Of course it turned out that my hernia was a baby; I was pregnant. I had no concept of what that would mean, so I just went home and gave the test results to Dad.

My boyfriend's parents arranged a meeting with Dad to discuss our situation. However Dad had already decided that I would keep the baby and he would support me in raising the child. My boyfriend's parents knew it was the wrong decision but they were powerless to stop us.

I had no-one to talk to about the pregnancy and didn't have regular checkups with the doctor, so I just continued on as normal. I went to school, played on the slides and swings at the park, climbed trees and acted as if nothing out of the ordinary was happening. I continued at school until two weeks before the baby was born and only finished then because it was the December school holidays.

One day I was out riding the trusty old bike that I had found on the rubbish. I was about eight and a half months pregnant, riding my little heart out. I came across my boyfriend's parents in their car and stopped to chat, asking if they knew where my boyfriend was.

I look back now and wonder what would have been going through their heads, seeing me riding along heavily pregnant without a care in the world. I eventually found my boyfriend at our hide out up in the tree house, so I hopped off my bike and scrambled right up there with him.

Right at the end of the pregnancy, my friends and I were walking through a shopping centre car park. I decided it would be funny to do a football leap onto the back of one of the girls. Little did I realise my friend could see my reflection in the shop window. She ducked when she saw what I was up to, and I went flying over the top of her and fell on the concrete, straight onto my heavily pregnant stomach. People came running from all over to help, but I just got up and acted like nothing had happened.

I suppose I didn't really comprehend what was happening to me.

My First Baby Arrives

I felt like my pregnancy was going on forever. I was so big but didn't feel too uncomfortable, even though I was days overdue. I was still very fit and was so desperate to have the baby that I organised a group of my friends to come jogging with me to bring the labour on.

The labour and birth are as clear in my memory as if they were yesterday. My boyfriend and my brother were hanging out in the shed with their friends while I was inside, playing the Nintendo 64. We went to bed at around eleven and just as I was climbing into the bed I felt warm water trickle down my legs. I said to my boyfriend 'I think I'm in labour, I can feel water running down my legs', to which he replied 'You've probably just wet yourself' and fell asleep.

Dad was in the lounge room watching TV so I went out to him and told him what was happening. He said 'Hell, let's go to the hospital'. I grabbed towels and put them between my legs, then made my boyfriend get up.

Dad had borrowed a car from his brother so my boyfriend, Dad, brother, stepmum and I started off to the hospital before Dad realised there was no petrol. While we waited at the petrol station we all bickered about who would be coming in to the birthing room with me. I was quite adamant that I didn't want my Dad or stepmum in the birthing room, which created an argument.

We eventually arrived at the hospital where I was put into a wheelchair and my brother wheeled me inside. I told my Dad, stepmum and brother to wait outside while I went into the birthing room with my boyfriend.

I tried to relax in the bath but all I felt like doing was vomiting. The back pain was getting really bad, so the nurses propped me up on the bed. I started screaming for my Dad and the nurses brought him, my stepmum and brother into the room. The nurse said that it was time for the baby to come so I needed to take my pants off. I refused. Of course they couldn't let me keep my pants on, so I made everyone leave the room while I removed them.

Everybody came back in as the baby started to come. I was screaming so loud that even the lady who shared my hospital room could hear me from the other end of the hospital. When the baby was born my boyfriend cut the cord and then the baby was given to my Dad. I don't know why Dad was handed the baby instead of me, but soon I had my chance to cuddle Josh for the first time.

At the beginning I don't remember feeling anything other than shock that I had a baby to look after. By day two of my hospital stay I was feeling lonely and scared. I walked around the hospital crying, not knowing what to do. I rang Dad from a pay phone sobbing, asking him to come and stay with me. My stepmum came and stayed with me for two nights. She didn't like me and I didn't like her, so when Dad made her stay with me at the hospital I didn't want her there, I wanted my Dad. Josh's birth was a turning point for us though and now I realise how much support she gave me through that time.

I left the hospital on Christmas morning and stopped off at a few friends' houses to show my baby off. Once home the challenge began; I had to learn how to bath and feed the baby.

This is Not the Life I Had Planned

Josh was born in the December school holidays. I had just turned sixteen. I struggled with looking after the baby so Dad, my stepmum and I all took turns getting up to him at night. Josh must have felt that I was not settled and would cry all night. My boyfriend was also only sixteen and he had no idea what was happening, let alone how to care for a baby.

Looking back, I realise that I may have had post natal depression, however in everyone else's eyes I was just an angry young girl. I tried my hardest to be the best Mum I could be with the few resources I had.

Dad's was a Housing Commission house, with people coming and going all the time. There was no routine and it was a very difficult environment to bring a baby into. There were so many dirty dishes stacked up in the kitchen that I couldn't sterilise Josh's bottles unless I cleared the dishes first.

It took me a long time to accept my new responsibility. Sometimes I would put Josh to sleep and go out the back to the shed to hang out with my friends. My stepmum would call me when he woke up but I was full of resentment, thinking 'Yeah so what, why don't you feed him?' I would bring Josh out to the shed to feed him, surrounded by my friends drinking, smoking and listening to loud music. I had no comprehension that a baby needed a beautiful, nurturing, peaceful feeding experience.

Dad and I argued quite a bit and after yet another fight I decided I would run away. I packed a few clothes and baby bottles into my baby bag and called a guy I knew. When I was thirteen he had been my first boyfriend. He was covered in tattoos and bashed people for sport, but he was also twentyone years old by then and had a car. I was desperate.

The guy took Josh and I back to his Mum's house. He had serious anger problems and that night during an argument with his Mum he threw the washing machine at her. Josh was screaming and I was scared but didn't know what to do. Dad had no phone and I was an hour away from home. So while the rest of the household was taking drugs and getting drunk I slept on the floor with my baby.

The next day his Mum offered to take the baby out for the day. I didn't even know this lady but I was desperate for a break so I let her take Josh. I have no idea where she took him or why she wanted to. I can only guess she knew her son was violent and didn't want him to hurt my baby.

Eventually after three nights I begged him to take me home. He drove me half way there and then kicked me out of the car. I was left on the side of the road with my baby and all our gear. I walked all the way home carrying Josh in my arms.

Soon the school holidays had finished and I was back into my routine, going to school, going to work and feeling good again. I took Josh to school with me and Dad would meet me at the café after school and take Josh so I could go to work. I even started to pay my little sister $5 each day to wash the baby bottles so that I could save time getting ready for school.

When I was eighteen I decided it was time to move out, as Dad and I had been arguing a lot and I couldn't stand living in a messy house. I love a clean home! By this time Josh had started walking and it had become too hard to take him to school, so I had dropped out of school and started work. Luckily my boyfriend went to school with a guy who worked at the real estate office, so we were able to get ourselves a little two bedroom unit.

When Josh was two I fell pregnant with my daughter Tahlia. I had my second child when I was nineteen, and once again worked up until a week before she was born. I started back at work only three days after the birth, and a few months later started a course at TAFE also.

My boyfriend also started working full time, and began an apprenticeship. We were both so young, with two little children to care for and both working and studying. This took its toll on our relationship and we decided to go our separate ways. He moved back with his beautiful family to their beautiful home.

Only a week later, my landlord announced she wanted to move into her unit. This meant I had to move out, but Dad's house was already full. I had absolutely nowhere to go and was given two weeks to vacate.

I asked a friend if I could stay at her house and promised it wouldn't be long until I found my own place. I didn't really mind too much about sleeping on her lounge room floor. She was the one I partied with most weekends, so I thought it would be fun as we could party all the time.

As the days and weeks went by, the excitement and fun disappeared. There was no mattress on her lounge room floor, just a blanket and pillow. I would cradle my four month old baby in one arm and my three year old son in the other. Sometimes to get a good night's sleep I would put them both to sleep on one of those fold-out kiddie lounges. It was June, and the gas had gone out all around Melbourne so it was freezing cold.

Do you remember someone at your school that you looked up to? One of those people who had a white picket fence family, someone you thought was so very lucky? One girl I was friends with at school had the lot. She was beautiful inside and out.

One night I had been staying over at Dad's for the night with the kids when Dad and I had another argument. It was 11pm when I grabbed the kids and ran out of the house. I was walking back to my friend's house to sleep on her floor, crying all the way. I couldn't believe what my life had turned into. All those dreams I had were turning into nightmares.

It was raining hard and I stopped at a corner near a streetlight, waiting to cross the road. A car pulled up and someone wound down the window and asked if I was ok. It was then I realised it was the same girl who I had looked up to all those years ago. I was horrified and extremely embarrassed. She asked me what the hell was I doing out in the rain with two babies in the middle of the night. I tried to explain and still can't forget the look on her face as I told my story. I suppose knowing me from our school days she wasn't too surprised that my life had descended to this.

When I finally got back to my friend's lounge room floor, I cried all night. I woke up the next morning to the beginning of a new journey. I called my ex boyfriend's Mum and asked if I could live with her. Of course they said they would take me in, but first I had decided to go out nightclubbing to numb my pain.

I arranged for Dad and my stepmum to look after Josh and Tahlia and out I went. Around that time I didn't just go out for the fun of it, I needed to find a man to live with; I was desperately searching for someone to love me and my children.

I did meet a man that night, and ended up in a relationship with him for many years. I was not emotionally stable when we got together, and had a lot of issues that I had not dealt with. Going into a relationship with a man like this just added fuel to an already existing fire. I don't want to lay blame solely on one person for what happened; I acknowledge that my head was not in the right place to be entering into an already unstable man's life. Add to that the stresses of bringing the children into the relationship, and we were like a tornado meeting a volcano. We were doomed to have a volatile relationship from day one.

I had bought a ticket on a roller coaster ride of violent and controlling behaviour that went on for many years and affected everyone it touched. As time went on, people became more and more concerned for my welfare and my children's safety, but I was so desparate to be loved that I stayed in the relationship and drew away from the people who spoke out against it.

Throughout the day my boyfriend would check on me at home or at work to ask who I had been talking to. He listened to all my phone calls and constantly accused me of having an affair. At first I actually enjoyed his jealousy. It felt as if someone cared about me. I became jealous of him also, so we lived in a constant state of mistrust and fear.

However the physical abuse soon followed and he would spit on me, call me names and abuse the kids. I was beaten in front of the children and it became a regular occurrence for Dad to be on call to pick up the kids after another violent episode.

Every day I was told I was a slut, I was dragged up like an animal not a human, I was ugly, I was fat, I was psycho, I was a horrible Mum, you name it I was called it. You can imagine what my self esteem was like.

I loved **to** spend hours reading books as this was the only thing I was given permission to do. I wasn't allowed to stay in touch with my friends and family. Every aspect of my life was controlled and if it hadn't been for my books I truly don't think I would be alive today.

My life had been consumed by the abuse, police, Department of Human Services, everything I used to watch in movies. I could not believe my life had come to this. It was just getting worse and worse.

I had become a very angry, unsettled person. I blamed myself for his violence towards me and my children. I had convinced myself that if I was a nice person he would be nice to me. It was no wonder he abused me, as I was angry all the time. It was not until I learnt about the cycle of domestic violence that I started to realise why I was so angry and learnt not to blame myself.

I had visited the hospital many times before, making various excuses for my injuries, but this time was different. This time it was one of my children who had been hurt, and now they would not let me take my children home.

There I was in that tiny room with my three children, the DHS, police and hospital staff, and they were talking about taking all my children from me and placing them in foster care. I was given an ultimatum; I could either keep the children or keep the violent relationship. I am so grateful to have been given my choices so clearly that night. Without having it laid on the table like that I probably just would have stayed in that relationship, surviving day to day, until, well, who knows.

So I started a twelve week program for victims of domestic violence, and learned about the cycle of violence. The build up, the explosion, the remorse and then the honeymoon, round and round it went. Without fail I would get sucked in again at the honeymoon stage and go back to him. I would start to see the build up happening and knew an explosion was just a moment away.

During the build up I would get angry and yell back at him and the kids would be left to fend for themselves. Then through the explosion it would become physical, with us both hurting each other. During the remorse stage I would be crying with my kids sitting on my lap. He would say things such as 'Well if you didn't get angry I wouldn't hit you.' I would promise not to get angry anymore and then while the kids and I were still crying he would say something like 'Let's go on a trip. We'll get a motel room and take the kids somewhere special.' For me this honeymoon phase was the most dangerous part, as I would always be tempted back with beautiful offers of rewards or love.

I became much stronger as I began to understand this cycle and decided I couldn't live with the game anymore.

Donna, the counsellor assigned to me through this process, was an amazing angel. I have tried many counsellors over the years and Donna was the best for me. She was straight to the point and didn't let me make excuses, just worked me hard without being fluffy. This was just what I needed; a straight shooter who would tell it as it is. Donna saw in me what I didn't, she believed in me when I didn't and she gave me the resources to change my life. Donna told me to start reading books and since I picked up that first book my life has never been the same.

I know the power a book can have when you really want to change your life and so I wanted to help others in the same way. I don't share my story so people will feel sorry for me, only to paint an example of how you can draw strength from your obstacles and still make your dreams come true.

Wow, I am Living my Dream Life

Through all the dramas that were happening in my life, I continued to visualise my dream life and took action along the way to make sure I was still on that path. Even though I was living in a situation so far removed from my dream, I still worked towards my goal.

When I was sleeping on my friend's floor with the children I would visualise that I had a beautiful home and was a successful business woman.

Now that I was clear about what I wanted, I set about achieving the small goals which would ultimately get me my dream job. I completed a business secretarial course at TAFE which allowed me to access the funeral industry through the work experience program. After a week at a funeral company on work experience, I was hooked.

From this point onwards everything was focused on getting into the funeral industry. I imagined myself wearing the company uniform, driving the hearse and helping the grieving families. It was as if I was already living my goal.

Once the wheels were in motion I began feeling really good about myself. At this time in my life I was living in a not-so-nice unit and driving a not-so-nice car. I wanted to live the way I felt, so every day I visualised my dream house and the car I would be driving.

Soon, when I was working full time as a trainee Accountant's Assistant, I realised I could finally afford to live in a nice house and buy a nice car. I set a goal that in six months I would be living over the hill in a nice estate. I wanted to be around people who shared my values and were family orientated and this estate seemed like the perfect place.

I went around the estate and found what looked like my ideal home. I knocked on the door and asked the lady who answered if she owned the property. She told me she was renting so I drove to her real estate and told the agent that in six months time I would like to rent the property. I asked him to call me when the tenant moved out, and a few months later the call came. My house was up for lease and I signed on the spot.

Now it was time to get the car to suit my house, so I test drove my dream car and within two months had found it for sale. It had only one lady owner and was the exact colour I had visualised.

Life just kept getting better and better. I was attending counselling twice a week, had a great job, a beautiful house and a nice car. My kids were happy and my life finally had a new meaning to it.

I was then ready for a dream partner to suit my dream life, so I created my very own Dream Partner Chart, with everything I desired in a partner.

This was my wish list:

I would love a partner who is over 35

I would love a partner who has no children

I would love a partner who has a stable job

I would love a partner who wears nice clothes to work

I would love a partner who has an office job

I would love a partner who loves children

I would love a partner who is ambitious

I would love a partner who has motivation and loves doing things

I would love a partner who looks after himself

I would love a partner who understands my ambition

I would love a partner who doesn't drink or smoke

I would love a partner who lets me be me

I would love a partner who is confident within himself

I was chatting with the girls in my office about the guys we worked with, talking about which ones we liked. One of the girls said that a guy named Dave was quite good looking and I clearly remember saying 'Really? I don't think he's attractive at all'. In the second breath I added 'I reckon Dave would be a wife basher'. I still had the idea that men were nice in front of people but behind closed doors they bashed their partners.

Dave often came into my office at lunch time and tried to talk to me. It really annoyed me as I loved to read my newspaper at lunch time and didn't like to be interrupted. I didn't want to be rude though, so would sit and listen to him. I knew Dave was married and wasn't interested in him at all.

One day he asked if I would like to take my kids and watch him go-kart. I said 'Um, aren't you married? I don't want to be rude but why would you want me and my kids to go and watch you go-kart?' It was then that Dave opened up to me, saying he was staying at a friend's place as he had separated from his partner. I kept saying no as I had no intention of getting involved with anyone I worked with, let alone Dave. I had no trust in men and was not interested at all. I believed that Dave was just another violent man.

I ended up talking to Dave a fair bit and got to know him quite well. Eventually I gave in and took my children to the go-kart track. I started to think he was a nice person but still couldn't quite understand. If he was such a nice guy, why would he want to be with a girl like me who had three children and lots of baggage? Although I had done so much work on myself I was still surprised he could see the qualities I had in me.

My children cried when I told them about him and said 'Mum, this man will just be like the other one. He'll be all nice to begin with and then he will start hitting you'. They begged me to not get involved with Dave. I sat down one night with Dave and talked about my own and my children's fears. I needed to know if he had any violent history and asked if he had ever hit his ex partner, whether he yelled and sweared at his ex, and how he argued with her. He must have thought I was crazy but it was so important to me – I couldn't put myself or my children through another violent relationship.

We started to spend time together, jogging and taking the kids to the beach. I couldn't believe this man seemed to be everything on my Dream Partner Chart. I eventually let things just flow and allowed the relationship to grow, and we have been together ever since. I can't say it's been easy; it took quite a while for all of us to totally trust him.

We now have two babies together, are engaged, live in our beautiful house, and together run a successful business. I still pinch myself at my new life and am really enjoying being a Mum this time round. This is a very new experience for me, and my babies are settled, content, and very happy.

If I can turn my life around from where I was to now living my dream life, so can you.

The Day I Discovered my Passion

I remember the day I discovered my passion as if it were yesterday. I was eight years old and walking to the milk bar for an ice-cream with Dad on a warm summer's night.

As we walked I saw flashing lights and heard the siren of a police car. Naturally I was curious and ran to see what was happening. There was a man bleeding to death in the middle of the road; he'd been hit by a car. I remember the police telling everybody to move away, but I stood there transfixed. It hit me that ten minutes before he had been a living, breathing human being and now he lay dead on the road.

The police put a white sheet over the body and Dad told me to come away. I wanted to stay and watch but Dad said no. I asked Dad what would happen to him and he said that a funeral director would arrange the burial. When I realised that there was someone who was responsible to care for this man after such a horrible death I knew I had found my passion. At the age of eight I knew I wanted to be a funeral director and eventually own my own funeral business!

From then on I started studying funeral directors, looking at funeral directors, reading about funeral directors. I even debated becoming a client of a funeral director to find out more!

When I was twelve we had moved from NSW to Melbourne and our new house was close to a well known funeral home. Whenever I passed the funeral home I imagined one day working there. My visions were so strong that I just knew I would make it happen.

When it came time to do my TAFE work experience I chose to work at a funeral director's. I began visiting funeral parlours regularly looking for work. One day I happened to walk into a local parlour just as the funeral assistant was going on six weeks' leave. I was so excited when they offered me the opportunity to work for six weeks in my chosen career.

My role was to clean the chapel, wash the hearses, and prepare the deceased for viewings. Each day on the board there would be a list of names of deceased people who needed to be dressed, made up and have their mouths sewn shut ready for viewing.

After a few days at work I came in to see that there were only four names on the board. I took my time and did a great job preparing two people as I knew I had time the next day to do the other two. When I was done I went home, but was shocked when I arrived the next morning to see around ten names on the board. I had three hours to prepare the first four people and put them into their coffins all on my own.

I took the challenge very seriously. I was dealing with someone's loved one, and was responsible to ensure they looked as natural as possible for the viewing. I managed to get everyone ready in time, and discovered through this how much better I work under pressure. I also learned a lot about the unpredictable nature of the funeral industry!

My most memorable moment was preparing a little four year old boy who had passed away. I spent so much time on this little boy, dressing him to perfection in the little suit his parents had prepared for him. He had blonde hair and blue eyes, just like my little four year old daughter at home. It was an incredibly confronting experience, and I slept with my little daughter every night for weeks afterwards. What a great lesson in how precious life really is. I learned so much from working in the funeral industry about keeping everything in perspective. I am constantly reminded that we only have one shot at life so we must make the most of it.

Finally after ten years of knocking on doors, writing applications, and weathering knock-backs I did get a full time position as a funeral director and was able to realise my passion. I really lived the motto NEVER EVER GIVE UP.

The irony of this is that only a couple of months after I became a funeral director I had to resign to help my son with the after effects of living in a violent relationship. However even this was a blessing in disguise as I am now running a successful business and also living another of my passions. Now I work with young Mums all over Australia to empower and inspire them to discover their passion and most importantly to make those passions a reality.

If you are powered by passion all things are possible!

OLD Life

Me growing up with my dad

Me aged 8, the year I discovered my passion

Me aged 9 the year I was sexually assaulted, I am the one with the dirty school uniform

Me aged 15 eight months pregnant mucking around in the shed I lived in

www.staceycurrie.com

Me aged 15 and nine months pregnant standing out the backyard of the housing commission home I grew up in

me aged 16 having just given birth to my first baby Joshua

Here I am aged 19 with my 3 year old and 4 month old. This is when we were homeless and sleeping on a floor.

This is the beating that changed my whole life. The day DHS and Federal police gave me my two choices

NEW Life

My partner Dave who gave me all the love I needed to spread my wings and live my dreams

me with my first born Josh aged 17 and my last baby Renee aged 2

Me aged 32 with my children Tahlia 13, Jack 11, Toby 3 and Renee 2

Me now as a motivational speaker

My business Brand Print Australia

Part Two

Action Steps

Discover Your Passion

Almost everyone, at some point in their lives, questions what life is about and why they are here.

Every person in the world, no matter who they are, has a purpose for being here, a calling. The work of your life is to discover that purpose and get on with the business of living it out. The only courage you need is the courage to find and follow your passion.

Does what you're doing with your life now feel exciting? Does it fill you up or leave you feeling empty and miserable? Forget what everyone else wants for you; what do you want?

Have you noticed that successful people often talk about passion? Sometimes we consider starting a business purely to make money, but if you are following your passion, money will naturally follow. Successful people have found the secret – if you are living your passion you feel so excited every day. It's like being on an enormous rollercoaster ride that you never want to get off.

Unfortunately, most people do not follow their passions in life. This can be due to creative blockage, fear or lack of money. True happiness only comes when you are doing what you're most passionate about. You have gifts to help others with, so what's holding you back? Why not overcome your obstacles, break through your fears and start pursuing your passion today?

Try this exercise to help you discover **what your true passion is:**

- Grab a pen
- Find a peaceful place where there is no access to email, laptop, mobile phone, kids etc

- When answering the questions, write the first answer that pops into your head. Be honest, and don't edit what you write or explain yourself, just use point form

- Make sure you write your answers down rather than just think about them

- Write as quickly as you can, preferably less than 30 seconds per question

- Don't allow any limitations or excuses. Imagine that you have all the money, time and resources you need to achieve what you want. Just let yourself fantasise.

What makes you feel excited? Think of activities, people, events, hobbies or projects. If it helps, ask yourself what you like to do. What do you get a kick out of? How do you have fun? If you were in a room with a whole lot of people and there were a few groups of people talking on different subjects, which group would you be most interested in joining? What would the topic be?

Think back to your childhood. What were you good at as a child? What were your favourite things to do?

What about now? What are you good at now? What are your favourite things to do?

What do you love about yourself?

_____

_____

What activities make you lose track of time?

_____

_____

What do you do that makes you feel great about yourself?

_____

_____

What interest, passion or desire are you most afraid of admitting to yourself and others?

_____

_____

What skills, abilities are you naturally good at?

_____

_____

What do your closest family and friends ask for your help with?

_____

_____

If you were a teacher for a day, what topic would you teach?

_____

_____

What are some obstacles you've overcome? How did you overcome them?

_____

_____

Who inspires you? These could be people you know or people you have never met. Think of family, friends, entrepreneurs, leaders, celebrities. What qualities inspire you the most in each person? Why do they inspire you?

_____

_____

Who do you know that's doing something you would like to do? Describe yourself doing this instead.

_____

_____

What do you regret not fully DOING, BEING or HAVING in your life?

_____

_____

If you could get your message out to thousands of people, who would those people be? What would your message be?

How could you contribute to make the world a better place for yourself and others?

What's stopping you from taking action to follow your passion?

Now is the time to really create a clear vision of your passions and possibilities. Let go of your inhibitions and have fun!

In this chart, list the passions that came out in the exercise above. Beside each passion, list the action steps you would have to take to achieve these fantasies.

My Passions	Action Steps I Would Need to Take

Now write a scene from your ideal life. Imagine that you are living your dream life now. Write exactly how your dream life looks, as if you are living it right now. Put in enough detail and description to make it seem very real

_____

_____

_____

_____

_____

_____

_____

_____

_____

_____

_____

_____

_____

_____

_____

_____

_____

_____

Now you have your ideal future in black and white in front of you, try coming back to it every few months. Once you are clear on what your true passion is, you will probably find that you start to head in the direction of your goals.

To live your best possible life and pursue your passions requires a lot of support and encouragement. Surround yourself with people who will support your dreams, be there for you in down times and celebrate your successes with you.

When you have passion for your work and life, you will naturally have so much drive, energy and motivation that you will be excited every day. You will be springing out of bed each morning, ready to face another day.

So now you know your passions and dreams in life, how are you going to start this exciting adventure? Most importantly, when are you going to take action to make it happen?

What Are Your Values?

Your values are the things that are most important to you, the rules you live by.

My number one value in life is my children; my second is health and third is success. When I was living in a terrible relationship, none of these values were being met. My children were unhappy, my health was not good and my success was on a constant roundabout. I was miserable.

If you are living your values you will feel contented and happy, but the opposite is also true. Your values do not lie. If you are not living your values, you can pretend to be happy – and to the outside world I looked as though I had it all. I was attractive and dressed well and my kids always looked very well cared for. However on the inside I just wanted to die.

Now that I have turned my life around and am living my values, my children are happy, my health is great and my career is where I dreamed it would be. I am finally contented and happy on the inside as well as the outside.

Are you contented and happy? Is your life consistent with your top three values? Do you know what your top three values are?

Your values are determined by everything that has happened to you in your life. The influence of your family and friends, your religious views, your education, your life experiences and many more factors have helped determine what is important to you. If you look at your life so far and the way you are living today, you will have a sense of what is important to you, what your values are.

Once you have defined your values you will begin to understand the impact they have on every aspect of your life. Your values are the key to successful decision making, contribution and interaction with people. Your values are your answer to achieving your goals and your life purpose.

You MUST live your values every day at work and at home. Living your values is one of the most powerful tools you can have. It will help you be the person you want to be, and the person you need to be in order to accomplish your goals and dreams, and to lead and influence others. Don't settle for anything less.

This exercise will help you learn the three essential values in your life. Keep these in mind as you go about your daily life, and ensure you are remaining faithful to them because they are the essence of who you are.

I was introduced to this exercise during the FIRE UP Coach Training and it blew me away. It was extracted from material designed by Marilyn Atkinson of Erickson College and used in their programs to explore values.

Possible Core Values:

Peace	Success
Wisdom	Integrity
Status	Love
Family	Friendship
Fame	Justice
Wealth	Influence
Power	Happiness
Authenticity	Truth
Joy	Spirituality

Identify special, peak moments when life was especially rewarding. Focus on the moment, not the details.

_____

_____

What was important about this moment? Using the list above, what were the values being honoured in the moment? What values were you living in this moment?

_____

_____

Think of times you were willing to get into trouble to achieve what you needed to. Look at the feelings and circumstances, and then flip it over. Is the other side of what you were feeling a value? Was there a value that pushed you to do what you did?

_____

_____

Think of times you were angry, frustrated or upset. Look at the feelings and circumstance, and then flip it over. Is the other side of what you were feeling a value?

_____

_____

Who are you when you are at your very best?

_____

_____

What qualities do you look for in a friend? What is important in these qualities?

_____

_____

If you were to live one day as an animal, which animal would it be? Why? What is important about being that animal?

_____

_____

If you were to live one year as a tree, what kind of tree would you be? Why? What is important about being that tree?

_____

_____

What must you have in your life to feel fulfilled beyond your basic needs? What are the values you absolutely must honour?

_____

_____

If you were stranded on a desert island...

- Which five books might you bring? What is important about these books?

1. _____

2. _____

3. _____

4. _____

5. _____

- Which five pieces of music might you bring? What is important about this music?

1. _____

2. _____

3. _____

4. _____

5. _____

- Which five objects might you bring? What is important about these objects?

1. _____

2. _____

3. _____

4. _____

5. _____

- Which five movies might you bring? What is important about these movies?

1. _____

2. _____

3. _____

4. _____

5. _____

- Which five friends might you bring? What is important about these particular friends?

1. _____

2. _____

3. _____

4. _____

5. _____

We all occasionally display obsessive behaviour. When we insist on something, when it is a case of 'my way or the highway' this is an obsessive expression of our values. Our friends and family may assist us by pointing these things out e.g. 'You are such a clean freak!' or 'You hog all the attention!' What do people tease you about? What drives them nuts about you? Focus on the value you are expressing, not just what you are doing.

Think of three people you deeply respect. Which one quality do you admire in each person?

On your deathbed after a life well lived, what would you tell your children are the three most important things you have learned in your life? Why were they so critical?

You sneak in the back door at your 100th birthday party and overhear people talking about you. What do you hope your friends, family and colleagues are saying about you?

What gives you the most joy, satisfaction and renewal in your life?
What is important about these things?

_____

_____

List your three top values:

1. _____

2. _____

3. _____

Create A Vision Board

*N*ow that you have discovered what your values and your passions are, it's time for fun. When someone first suggested to me to make a vision board I thought it was a load of garbage. I couldn't see how doing a craft project could possibly make any difference to my life. I was absolutely amazed when I looked back at an old vision board I came across last year and saw everything I had put on my board in 2007 had actually been achieved. At the time I made that board I can remember thinking 'There is no way I can do these things, I have no money'. And yet I did it anyway. The fantasies I had on my 2007 vision board were:

- A bright blue Ford Territory (I bought one only a year later)

- Do a boot camp (I now have my fitness and my body back)

- Own my own home near the beach (I recently purchased my first home near the beach)

- Have five employees working in our business (we now have five employees)

It's amazing how powerful vision boards can be. All these goals seemed like fantasies at the time, and yet once I had them clearly in front of me, my life and my focus seemed to start moving towards them.

A vision board could very well transform your life forever. It is a tool that allows your mind to create the life you dream of. Hang your vision board somewhere you will see it every day. You will be amazed how your goals will come to life.

Before you begin, ask yourself a few questions:

- What do I want?

- What is my desired outcome in life?

- What would it look like?

- If I had this life how would I feel?

What you need to create a vision board:

- A large piece of cardboard

- A glue stick

- Some old magazines/books

- An unlimited imagination

How to make your vision board:

- Grab the magazines and cut out pictures that show dreams you have for your life. You might see pictures of material things such as cars, clothes and holiday destinations, or it might be pictures of the personal life you desire, such as wedding scenes or children. Maybe it will be pictures of people working in the career you aspire to. This is your personal vision board so it needs to reflect the life you imagine for yourself.

- Take the picture that is the most important to you and glue it right in the middle of your cardboard. My greatest goal was to have a happy family so I glued an enormous happy family photo right in the middle of my cardboard.

- Around the central picture, glue the other pictures of all the dreams you have.

- Allow your mind to imagine anything it chooses. Don't limit yourself by thinking 'Oh but I can't afford it'. Imagine you have all the money, time and support you need, then what would your life look like?

Let your mind explore….

You can use your vision board to bring your partner or family into your dream. Sit down with them and show them your vision board. Explain what your goals and visions are for your life. This can really help them understand where you are trying to get to and it will be easier for them to support you. They might even like to make their own vision board.

If you can get into the habit of supporting each other you can set goals together and make them happen. Remember to celebrate any goals you achieve together! This helps to build your self esteem and also shows your partner that you care enough to support one another's dreams. Once you start seeing the results of the process you will become better partners, parents and lovers. The biggest key to this however is ACTION.

Goal Setting and Action Taking

You have to sit by the side of a river a very long time before
a roast duck will fly into your mouth

Guy Kawasaki

Have you been dreaming of your ideal life? Have you attended the seminars, read the books, listened to the CDs but still find yourself waiting for 'it' to happen? Why keep waiting? Decide to move forward, set a goal and take action on it and you will be unstoppable. Today is action day, start now and all your dreams will come to life.

What is it that you would like to achieve in the near or distant future? Success in your career? Losing those unwanted kilos? Buying that dream car? Gaining greater confidence? Having more energy? Being in a fulfilling relationship? Buying your first home?

Whatever it is that you want, the first step is to set a goal. Goals keep you focused and motivated, and increase your likelihood of getting the outcome you want.

Every time you conquer a goal your self esteem rises. When you next come across a situation that you once would have found stressful, your previous success will give you the confidence to overcome your obstacles. Your whole outlook on life becomes happier and everything seems more exciting.

Once you have set your goal, action will be your key to unlock the door to success. There is no point having goals written out and stuck on the fridge and then wondering why nothing changes.

BE-DO-HAVE!

Who do you need to be to get what you want?
What do you need to do to get it?
What is it you will then have?

It takes a lot of action to run a business, raise five children, keep a partner happy and also keep fit. But I know that if I want to get everything I desire from life, I need to actually make it happen. I had many mentors around me, a fantastic counsellor, Dad telling me I could do anything I dreamed of, a boss giving me advice, and a trainer to tell me how to keep fit. But I was the only one who could take action on all this information. No one could do it for me, I had to get off my butt and do it myself.

Think about some of the things that you would like to achieve. What excuses do you have for not achieving your desired outcome? What actions are you NOT taking? What actions could you be taking? Imagine for one minute that you took action to make it happen. How would that make you feel? How would your life be different?

I have always wanted to feel fit and healthy. Like many Mums I put on unwanted kilos during pregnancy. I have to admit I really didn't enjoy being pregnant at all. I didn't like being so big, not just because of the way I looked but because I had no energy and couldn't do things quickly any more. Through each of my five pregnancies I have always set a goal to lose weight after the baby was born.

When I was younger I preferred the quick fix approach. I would starve myself, take diet pills, do whatever it took to lose those kilos. I did lose the weight but I also became a very moody, angry mother and when I did eventually start eating again, the weight piled back on.

Once I got a little older and wiser, I decided to lose weight the healthy way. I set small goals before the baby came so that I was prepared. My baby was born in July, so my small goals looked like this

- By August 10th I have lost 3kgs. I am walking for 40 minutes six days a week and eating six healthy meals a day.

- By September I have joined a boot camp. I attend one hour sessions three days a week and have now lost 6kgs; I am still eating six healthy meals a day.

- By November I have lost 10kgs and fit into my Melbourne Cup dress. I still attend boot camp and eat healthy meals.

Because the goals were small and manageable, I was able to achieve them easily. I took action and WOW did I look good in that bright blue mini dress on Melbourne Cup day.

Make your goals S.M.A.R.T.

Specific, Measurable, Achievable, Realistic, Timely

In order to reach your goals, firstly you must be really clear on what it is you are trying to achieve.

Ask yourself 'What do I want?' List the top five goals you have been putting off that you really want to accomplish. Write them as if you have already accomplished them. For example: I have lost 10kgs and am now wearing my sexy black mini dress.

1. _____

2. _____

3. _____

4. _____

5. _____

From this list, select the one goal that is your highest priority, the one that you would most regret if you didn't achieve it in your life. Write down that number one goal and set a date it will be accomplished.

My number one goal: _____

Goal Date: _____

How will I know when I have achieved it?

_____

Now you will need an action plan to take you towards your goal. Have a look at the example, and then create your own.

GOAL ACHIEVMENT PLAN

What do I want to achieve? I want to lose 10 kgs by November 3rd	
Why do I want to achieve this goal? I want to be fit and healthy. I want to look good and feel good in my clothes and have more energy	
What are the actions and commitments I need to make to achieve this goal?	
1st action step - Walk every night	I will commit to- Walk five nights a week for 45 minutes each night Mon, Tues, Wed, Thur and Friday.
2nd action step - Eat healthier	I will commit to- Cut out all fried and fatty foods. Eat six small proportion healthy meals each day.
3rd action step - Drink water everyday	I will commit to- Drink two litres of water each day
4th action step - Get enough sleep	I will commit to- Go to bed at 9.30pm every night and get up 5.30am every morning
5th step action- Play a sport	I will commit to- Play tennis every Saturday with Sally
6th step action- Join a boot camp	I will commit to- Sign-up for boot camp sessions

When do I want to achieve this goal?
November 3rd

What obstacles and excuses can I expect?
Too tired after work to go for a walk
Too cold or hot to walk
Too lazy – can't be bothered to make a healthy meal
Lack of time
Nobody to look after the kids

What are the solutions to the obstacles?
Get up earlier and go for a walk before work
Prepare meals at night for the following day
Create time by not watching TV at night
Wear a jumper and beanie when walking
Walk later at night when it is cooler
Join a gym
Take the kids with me in their pram or on their bikes
Visualise my super sexy size 10 body each and every night and morning
Put a picture of a super sexy size 10 bikini babe on the fridge

Goal Achievment Plan

What do I want to achieve?	
Why do I want to achieve this goal?	
What are the actions and commitments I need to make to achieve this goal?	
1st action step -	I will commit to-
2nd action step -	I will commit to-
3rd action step -	I will commit to-
4th action step -	I will commit to-

5th step action-	I will commit to-

6th step action-	I will commit to-

When do I want to achieve this goal?

What obstacles and excuses can I expect?

What are the solutions to the obstacles?

Commit and Persist for Success

A great leader knows that success requires a HUGE amount of commitment.

Not having anyone support me or become excited for me as I was growing up led me to become very competitive. In turn, this desire to achieve taught me that I had to be fully committed in order to see my plans through.

Every year in the cross country race at school I would come in second place. I competed in the regional and then the state cross country races, but Dad only attended once as he worked a lot. A teacher or someone else's parent would have to take me to each event.

There was another girl who I could never beat; she was the one who came first every year. At the race, her Mum, Dad, Grandma, Grandpa, Aunts and Uncles would all be cheering her on, yelling 'C'mon you can do it! Run faster!'. Mind you this girl would practise and practise every afternoon. I never practised; I just went with the flow and tried my hardest on the day.

I was determined to beat this girl and eventually after coming second so many times I blitzed her in the 800m running event. Although I don't need other people's approval, I still feel that small sadness at not having anyone to celebrate my win with. I did feel an incredible sense of achievement at persevering until I reached my goal, and continue to apply this level of commitment to every goal I have.

When I was completing my traineeship I finished months ahead of time simply because I had committed myself to excellence. This was no simple task with three children to get up, ready and off to day care and school each day. I would arrive at work an hour early each day and take work home to finish at night when the kids were in bed.

At the same time I was also heavily involved in my son's basketball and football, so I didn't even go out on the weekend. I had finally given up my weekend drinking and partying as I didn't want to waste my precious time with a hangover the following day. My son's football team must have noticed my commitment to the football club also as I was offered the role of their first-ever female football club president. I had to think long and hard about this decision but because I was completing my business traineeship, I decided to let this opportunity go. I knew I could not commit 100% to each thing.

The payoff for my focus and commitment was that I finished my traineeship with top grades and my work was kept as an example for other students. I was even nominated for the State Training Awards. I knew my results were a reflection of my hard work and commitment.

We have also made a commitment to our business from day one. We worked really hard to get the business to a point where we could train our employees to fill our roles. This has allowed us the time to focus on the more important issues.

Small steps will eventually lead you to your goal but first you must make a commitment and stick to it.

1. **Make time every morning to plan in advance**

   Each day, take a clean sheet of paper and make a list of what you will take action on that day to move you towards conquering your top goal. Make a list of ten tasks each morning. At the top of the list, put the task you really do not want to do, the one which always ends up in the too hard basket. This is probably the one which you have used for far too long as an excuse as to why you haven't been able to achieve your goal. If you get that task done first, the other tasks will seem simple and you will start to get excited.

2. **Learn how to apply Pareto's Principle, the 80/20 rule**

   Twenty percent of your daily activities will account for 80 percent of your results. If you focus 80 percent of your time and energy on the top twenty percent of your tasks, you will really see results. It's not just working smart that is the key; it is working smart on the right things.

Focus only on the high priority tasks that will ultimately lead you to your desired results.

3. Always begin your day with an organised and clutter free desk

As you start your day, be sure to have all your materials, equipment and notes that you need to work with. Being organised when you begin cuts out a lot of time later searching for essential items.

Always insist on working in a clean environment and you will feel more organised, efficient and fresh.

4. Set deadlines for each task

Every task needs a deadline. Commit yourself to ensuring you complete your task within your deadline. Stick to it and be tough with yourself, then reward yourself for a job well done when you accomplish it within the deadline.

5. Get things done fast

Don't waste time thinking too much about what needs to be done, just start it and finish it. Procrastinating and getting side-tracked account for many missed deadlines. If you move quickly and stay focused you may find that tasks that you thought would take six hours only take you two hours. The faster you move the quicker you accomplish your tasks. You will be amazed at how much more you can achieve if you stay on task and move fast.

The same rule applies throughout life. If you see an opportunity, take action immediately. Don't wait for it to land on your lap, move quickly and grab it while you can.

6. Take away all interruptions

Are you one of those people who can't seem to get anything done in time? Do you lose time making phone calls and answering emails? Begin your focused day with your phone off, email off, internet off (unless you are using it solely for your task). This is a must. I tested myself with this and could not believe the amount of time I wasted on email, phone and internet. Now when I am focused I stay 100% focused. Of course you do need to attend to emails and phone calls, so block a time out in the day that will be for this purpose. Then turn everything off again and get back to your task. Set aside days where you have nothing that will interrupt you all day.

The key to your success is your 100% commitment. Don't be surprised if you only half commit and only end up with half the results achieved.

Make today the beginning of your long term commitment to achieving this goal.

Surround Yourself With Positive People

As a teenager, it seemed that all we did was hang around bitching about whichever of our friends wasn't there at the time.

During yet another relationship break up, I would visit my friend every day. I would moan to her about how much of a nasty person my ex was, and she would tell her story of how bad her ex was. It would go on like this for months and months, day after day, blaming our ex's and other people for our misery.

Then I started to see Donna, the counsellor who was helping me move on from my break up. Donna was the same counsellor that had told me to read books, a suggestion that has changed my life in so many ways. With her help I went back to work and also began to attend a women's group counselling session twice a week. Donna was also giving me tasks to do at home so that I could move forward from my past bad relationship into a happy healthy one.

One of the tasks Donna set me was that every night before bed I was to write down the things that had made me feel happy during the day. The effect was amazing; once I began to see that in fact there were some good things happening in my life alongside all the bad things, I seemed to become more grateful for all the good stuff and stopped focusing so much on the bad stuff.

As this task started to take effect on me, I began to feel happier being with my kids. This was very new to me, as while I was in the volatile relationship it was extremely difficult to enjoy my kids. I was always so focused on yelling, fighting, and just getting through another day, as I was always angry in the relationship. I finally stopped focusing on my ex and started to see that I could be a fun, loving Mum. I would dance around with my kids and really spend quality time with them. The kids and I began to sit at the dinner table talking to each other instead of yelling.

My kids began to bond with me more and would cuddle up to me on the lounge. It was beautiful to have this in our lives after it had been missing for so long while we were living in the violence. I started to wake up in the morning feeling like the best Mum in the world, and my dreams and passions came back to me.

I began to eat only healthy food and drink water, and put sticky notes with positive affirmations all around my house. After a while my confidence and self esteem were so high, positive people actually enjoyed being around me.

Every night after work I would take my kids jogging in their pram. Soon the exercise and new focus meant that my body started to look fabulous. I then felt the need to dress that fabulous body in nice clothes. Everything in life seemed to roll in a more positive direction just from doing these simple tasks. The best part of it was that most of it didn't cost me a cent.

I was still regularly visiting my friend for coffee and a chat. I would knock on her door all pumped and ready for the day, but by the time I left I would feel drained and depressed. I couldn't quite put my finger on what was going wrong, however after a few months of feeling like this I realised that I was allowing her to suck the positive energy out of me. It was time to cut ties and move on.

Ten years later that friend of mine is still having the same old dramas about the same old topics we used to sit and whinge about all day long!

Once I had this awakening, I decided to do a little exercise. I wrote a list of all of my friends at the time. In one column I wrote the positives about that friendship and in another column for the negatives. I couldn't quite believe the outcome; not one of my friends brought anything positive or valuable into my life. That was when I made the decision to clean out my friends and replace them with fresh, happy, positive friends. It took until I was twenty two to achieve this, but the results were worth it.

Positive Friend Finder

Friend's Name	Positives	Negatives

Dealing with Loneliness

This was one of the very first lessons I learnt on my journey to success. One of my mentors told me 'the higher you go up in life, the lonelier it is'. What a true statement I found this to be.

When I was living in a chaotic world full of drama, homelessness and low self worth, I had lots of company in my misery. People would call or visit every day to hear all about the latest disaster I had created. My life was like one of those awful TV series; my fans couldn't wait for the next episode and I was the star of the show. When I eventually decided I'd had enough of this life and was ready to create my dream life and pursue my passion, my daily drama episodes stopped and my fans dropped away.

You attract people to you who are similar to you and I had been attracting people who lived their lives in a constant state of negativity and drama. The quality of my friendships was not solid or positive. I knew that if I was to succeed I had to make a clear choice. I had to move away from these people and find positive friends. However when I cleared out the negative people I realised I had no positive friends at all and started to get extremely lonely.

It became clear that in order to attract the friends I wanted I had to become a person I would like to be friends with. I made the decision that I would work on myself for one year before I made any new friendships. You can imagine what a lonely year that was. I knew it would be worth it though, because if I wanted to live a positive life I must surround myself with positive, like-minded people.

What really helped me through those tough times was a new group of women who gathered once a week to support each other in our common goal to create a positive life for ourselves. I thought of it as my 'positive like-minded group'.

If you are feeling lonely and want to make new positive friendships, I would strongly recommend that you start a local group like this. Its amazing how many lonely people are out there, sitting at home dreaming of making friends. They would love to be a part of a group like this, but maybe don't have the knowledge, skills or self confidence to make it happen. All it takes is one person to get the ball rolling. It's not hard to set up but it does take time and commitment.

This could be your chance to become a leader. You have the chance to show others the way, and be the expert who guides others rather than just another person waiting for someone else to take the lead. You can show that anyone can do this and empower others to do the same. True leaders inspire others to come to the top with them, and are not afraid of competition. They are not fearful when their followers become leaders themselves. This is what being a leader is all about.

STEPS FOR SETTING UP A GROUP

Clarify what the purpose of your group is

I had been looking for a young Mums' group to join, but found them to be quite rare. I wanted to make new friends, have my children socialise with other children, and surround myself with like minded Mums who were experiencing the same issues I was, one of which was loneliness. Parenting is such an important and rewarding job however young Mums are often under-prepared and under-supported. I wanted this group to focus on creating a positive life filled with goals and dreams for ourselves and our children.

Marketing the group (finding people to come along)

* Put flyers in local shop windows

* Put an ad in the local newspaper

* Do letterbox drops of invitations. Many lonely people are sitting at home all day and would love to receive an invitation

- Ask local childcare centres to put flyers on their front desks or windows

- Use the local phone book to call people who are in your target group

- Put a banner up where the local community will see it.

What are the group's values?

The values I was looking for in my group were:

- Support each other with personal and parenting challenges

- Promote positive talk amongst the group

- Encourage the children to play happily together

- Build self-esteem and confidence by helping each other feel valued

- Be there for each other in the good times as well as the tired, grumpy moments

- Nurture friendships and make a point of going out together sometimes without the children.

Costs

When we first began we would take it in turns to meet at each other's houses. Everyone brought a plate of food to share so the cost was quite low. If you choose a venue that charges for the space, you could share the costs amongst the group.

Venues

However as the group grew we started to meet in local coffee shops. You might also be able to use a room at the local community centre for a low cost. Make sure you choose a venue that is centrally located and near public transport, to make it easy for people to attend.

You will need to arrive early to set up the tables and chairs and check that the air conditioner or heater is on. Food is a highlight at any meeting, so organise some cakes, sandwiches or biscuits. Choose something simple, and remember that most people don't mind bringing a plate. Tea and coffee are a must, so check if your venue has equipment for this, or bring it along yourself. You could also consider background music to help people feel more relaxed.

Time

If the members of your group are parents, you will need to hold meetings either within school hours or in the evenings when one parent may be home to look after the children. Hold the meetings on the same day and time each week, to make it easy for people to remember.

Facilitators

What topic will you be talking about at each meeting? At my group we didn't use facilitators we just talked amongst ourselves. If you wanted to put on fantastic sessions with a new topic each week, such as goal setting or letting go of fears, you could bring in a speaker who has a lot of experience in this field.

A cost-effective idea might be to delegate one person from the group to prepare the next week's session. That person would be responsible for researching their topic and presenting it to the group the next week, followed by a group discussion on the topic. This not only helps build self esteem through learning new skills, but also keeps people accountable for their role in the group.

Resources

If you have handouts, folders etc, ensure that you have these prepared and photocopied in advance. When you arrive at the venue, put the resources out for each member, and set up any audiovisual equipment. Once the meeting starts you want everything to run smoothly rather than rummaging through your files for a handout at the last moment.

Welcome and introductions

Most people feel anxious and shy when they first join a group. To be a great leader you must make sure everyone feels at ease.

At the first session, introduce each person to the room as they arrive. It's a great idea to have a name tag for each person. Give the group time on this first day to chat to each other and settle in. Next you will need to let everyone know where the facilities are such as toilets, coffee and tea etc.

Start the first session off with a conversation such as 'Tell us one thing we would be surprised to know about you'. Go around the room leaving a minute for each person to answer. This brings everyone together and helps people feel at ease and comfortable with each other.

At each regular session, open with a question such as 'How has your week been?', 'What has been a positive learning experience for you this week?' or 'What has been your win this week?' Go around the room, giving each person two minutes to talk.

At the end of the session you could go around the room again, asking 'What did you like least and most about the session?'. This feedback will help guide you in your planning to ensure your group is meeting everyone's needs.

Ground rules

All groups need a set of ground rules. Grab a paper and pen and ask the attendees what they need to feel comfortable in this group.

Most people won't engage at first, for fear of saying the wrong thing. Give them some prompting and encouragement with suggestions such as:

- Do not interrupt the person who is speaking

- What we talk about is confidential

- Accept that we are all different

Remember many people may not have experience with being part of a group like this and they may find it quite daunting to begin with. Keep it real and make it fun and they will soon be looking forward to each session.

Contact details

Make a form in advance for everyone who is comfortable to share their contact details.

Details they may wish to share are:

- Name
- Address
- Email Address
- Phone Number
- Facebook Page

In any group some people will drop off and others will stay on and can even become life-time friends. All it takes is for one person to take charge, be the leader and encourage and motivate others. The others will be grateful for your assistance in helping them when they needed it most.

Fitting it all in

From around the age of six, I was pretty much responsible for myself. I was living with my Dad and stepmum however Dad worked at three jobs and my stepmum was frequently in hospital for months at a time.

This is probably where I learnt my organisational skills. From the age of eight I would get myself up and ready each morning and then walk myself to school. I had to learn exactly what time to get up and what time to leave. I was doing my own washing and also looking after my brother and sister. The household was extremely disorganised with no routine whatsoever. Sometimes dinner would be at 7pm, other times it would be 10pm, sometimes not at all.

By the time I had my son Josh at sixteen I was already an experienced Mum after looking after my brother and sister for so many years. I knew from a young age that I wanted my own business, so even though I had Josh I knew that I would have to finish school so I could go on to set up my business. I didn't want Josh to be an excuse for not achieving my goals.

I had to establish a routine to make this happen. I started to get up two hours earlier to get myself ready and Josh bathed and fed. I would then walk to school with Josh in his pram. When Josh started to walk it became too difficult to have him in the classroom, so I enrolled in a Business Secretarial Certificate II at TAFE. I was also working part time as a waitress, so I got plenty of practice at learning the skill of balancing work and life.

By the time my third baby arrived at the age of twenty one I thought I had mastered the art of balance. I was out of bed every morning at 5.30am, working fulltime as an Accountant's Assistant as well as completing Certificates II, III and IV in Business Administration Management. After this I went on to work full time as a Funeral Arranger/Conductor.

Now I am a Mum of five children and manage to have it all; run a fulltime business, exercise each day, eat healthy food, and spend time with my children and partner. It's not easy, however if I stay on top of everything, I manage it all. Every day for me is organised so I can fit in all that I want to achieve.

My day begins at 5.00am when I get up and sterilise the baby bottles. The babies wake at 6.00am so once they are up and dressed I have a shower. Then I get my older kids out of bed and Dave and I feed the babies. I have my own breakfast and clean the house before dropping the older kids at school. If my house and office are clean I feel more organised and on top of things. When I arrive at work I get straight onto my action lists. I don't do anything else until my whole list is ticked off, to ensure that I am always taking action towards my desired outcome of having a successful business.

When I arrive home from work I start in the kitchen, cooking dinner and preparing lunches for the next day. Then I wash the school uniforms and get everything ready for the next morning. One of the tricks I use is to get the tasks I loathe out of the way first and do them as fast as I can. I don't even think about it, I just do it. I know that if I work quickly I can spend more time with my children, so this keeps me moving. I don't watch TV as I would prefer to spend the time talking and playing with my children. I also want to stay fit and healthy so when the babies were small I even managed to go to boot camp three mornings a week before work. Now I often take the babies for a jog in the pram in the evening once I have finished all my tasks.

Being an extremely organised working Mum has also enabled me to complete a few other courses which I know will eventually lead me closer to my passions and dreams. I completed the FIRE UP Coach Training Program, which is an ICF accredited, NLP based coach training program. I also completed a Toastmasters public speaking course and many other seminars and programs.

Finding a way to balance work and life also helped me to move away from my negative family and friends. I wanted to feel fresh and healthy and so I had to introduce a healthy life style. To have a successful ongoing work life balance requires your mind, body and soul to be healthy.

Try these tips to living a balanced life:

- Wake up an hour before you have to. If you need to be out of bed at 7.00am, get up at 6.00am. You can get so much more accomplished with just one extra hour.

- Have the morning's tasks organised the night before ie: school uniforms and work clothes ironed, house clean, lunches made etc.

- Make sure you find time for exercise each and every day. One hour a day is a must; you need ME time.

- Eat healthy food. Unhealthy foods make you feel sluggish; eating healthily makes you feel GREAT!!

- Have dinner organised before you leave for work so that when you arrive home it takes half the time to make. Invest in a slow cooker to make this easier. You can use the time you save for exercise.

- Always serve dinner at the table with the family. To make it fun we play Happy Day, Bad Day. We go around the table and tell a story of one bad part of the day and one happy part of our day. This allows the kids to get things off their chest if something didn't go well for them, and also celebrate their successes.

- If you are a single parent, take the kids for a walk around the block. They will probably complain at the start however after a while they absolutely love the time spent talking with you.

- If you are a business owner, treat yourself like an employee. Start and finish at the same time every day and pretend you have a boss that is on your shoulder; it's amazing how much more effort you put in.

- Always dress like a business person, even if you work from home. When you feel and look great, your confidence raises and it rubs off on people.

- Have a working bee once a month and de-clutter your home and office. You will be amazed at how much more organised you feel when your home is organised.

- Spend time with your partner alone at least once a week. If you are lucky enough to have babysitters, organise a night out. Go for dinner, a walk, even bowling. If you can't go out, put the kids to bed an hour earlier once a week, turn the TV, laptops and computers off and have a good old yarn.

Now make a list of all the excuses you thought of while you were reading. What can you do to have it all?

I would love...	My excuse for not doing this is...	What can I do differently to make it happen...?

You Are the Most Amazing Person

*L*et's get one thing straight... everybody, at some stage in their life, lacks self belief. I grew up in awe of great business leaders; I studied them, I read their work, I watched them speak, I found all I could out about them.

One day I was invited to a business group with some of those leaders. We sat around the table going through our business plans and discussing obstacles. I could not believe my ears when I heard these business leaders talking about their challenges. They were experiencing the same challenges I was! I began to wonder if perhaps these people were actually human, just like me. Then it hit me... We ALL have self belief issues, the trick is in learning to acknowledge it, get over it, and move on.

One of the differences between successful people and unsuccessful people is that the successful people don't allow their self doubts and negative thoughts to consume them. They learn to develop a strong belief in themselves by retraining their negative thoughts into positive thoughts. It's as easy as that!!

If you would like to believe in yourself more strongly, try these tips. They really do work if you take action to make them happen:

Positive self talk

Tell yourself you are a BRILLIANT person. You look so good in that outfit. Pat yourself on the back when you make a great decision at work. Acknowledge your beautiful hair when you come from the hairdressers. ALWAYS make a habit of complimenting yourself, don't wait for others to tell you how wonderful or beautiful you are.

Make it a habit to make yourself feel special. If you keep relying on feedback from others you'll lose your own self belief.

When I was nineteen a woman told me I had ruined my life and would never amount to anything. I replied that I believed I was going to have a great business and own my own home by the age of twenty five. I was shocked that from the outside it appeared that my life was still a mess. I understand now that she could only see where I was at the time, and how I appeared to her. She couldn't see the self belief, determination, strength and vision that I had. If I had taken on what she said, I could have stopped my journey right there.

A similar thing happened when I was going out to lunch with my colleagues after a week at a new job. As we were leaving the office car park I was admiring the CEO's beautiful car and said 'I'm going to be a CEO of a company one day'. The other people in the car fell silent as they looked at the skinny twentyfour year old in the back seat with three kids at home. Four years later when I left the company, my goodbye card was filled with messages about the success that awaited me and wishing me luck with my business ideas.

Who you are today is not who you have to settle for being forever. Once people see you walking your talk, they will start believing you too, but you must believe in yourself first.

Be grateful

As we strive further and aim higher, we are constantly reminded what we do not have yet. Although we want more and more, we must also remember to value what we already have. If you aren't grateful for what you already have, what is the point of having more?

When you take the time to realise what you have already, it can really give a sense of achievement. All the hard work you are doing is already paying off, it IS working. And this can help motivate you to achieve even more.

When life isn't going well it can be hard to find anything to be grateful for, but there is always something. Having food to eat, the love of your family, a car to drive; all these are precious and worth acknowledging.

Every morning when you get out of bed, think of five things you are grateful for. Try 'I am so grateful to have such nice clothes to wear, I am so grateful my eyes are blue, I am so grateful I am an intelligent woman' etc. This will seem like all fluff and mirrors at the beginning but it REALLY does work.

Focus only on what you want, not what you don't want

Unfortunately many of us spend time focusing on the things we don't want in our lives. This is why we get what we don't want. Once you start focusing on what you do want, you will attract it.

Start paying attention to your thoughts; are they negative or positive? If a negative thought comes into your mind, acknowledge the bad habit and replace it with a positive, for example if you want to try something new and wonder 'What if they think I am stupid?' Acknowledge the negative thought and then say 'What others think of me is none of my business. Of course I am smart enough to do this'.

Negative people - move away, far away

Everyone has someone negative in their lives, we all do. However you do not have to tolerate negative behaviour. It is YOUR choice to be a part of it. You attract people who are similar to you and if you are negative you attract negative people. On the other hand if you are positive you attract positive people.

It is incredible the quality of people that come into your life once you discover the positive lifestyle. Imagine the difference if everyone around you got excited for you and supported your dreams. You will notice a huge difference in your self belief when you are surrounded by like-minded people.

Want positive? Be positive

Are you the positive person in your friend's lives, or are you the whinging whining negative friend?

If you desire a future of your dreams you MUST retrain your mind to think positive thoughts.

It is hard at the beginning to retrain your mind to constantly think positively, however it is possible to do a little each day to change the way you think. Whenever you think of something negative, acknowledge it, write it down then replace it with a positive thought. At the end of the day, take a look at the list. Count how many negative thoughts you had that day. After a couple of weeks it will become a habit to grab that negative thought as it comes along and quickly turn it to a positive thought. Choose only to see the good in life.

Making a list with each goal you wish to achieve will not only make them happen faster, but as you tick each one off as ACHIEVED, your self belief will sky rocket.

I am	*I am a motivational speaker*
I value	*I value inspiring and empowering people and helping them realise their dreams*
I can do	*I can do a fantastic workshop to empower many women*
I will	*I will begin writing my workshop plan*
Where (location)	*Grand Central Hotel*
When (date)	*Tuesday 3rd March*

This list will help to keep you accountable. If you don't keep yourself accountable, you will have the opportunity to use excuses for not achieving what you set out to do. After that wears off, you will begin to feel useless and stupid, then it all starts again. To achieve a greater self belief you must change the way you do things today.

No more excuses, get started and make it happen…

I am	
I value	
I can do	
I will	
Where (location)	
When (date)	

Dealing with Fear

We all have fears, every one of us. What really makes the difference is how you acknowledge your fears and what you do to get over them.

After working for ten years towards my goal, I was finally offered my dream job as a Funeral Arranger/Conductor. Unfortunately at the same time I was extracting myself from a terrible relationship. The police were involved and the children and I had plenty of scary nights.

After only three weeks at my new career, the phone rang on my way to work. It was my ten year old son, yelling that he refused to go to school; he hated life and wanted to kill himself. Working in the funeral industry, I didn't take his words lightly.

I called a friend and begged them to drive to my house and stay with my son until I got home. Then I called in sick to my brand new dream job and drove home so fast I'm surprised I didn't get booked.

When I got home, my son was yelling, kicking and screaming. He didn't want to go back to school and ended up being at home for the next week. I contacted a counsellor who told me that often in a violent domestic situation, once the perpetrator leaves the house the child feels safe enough to act out all the anger they had bottled up inside. This is what was happening to my poor son, he was just venting his frustrations after living in a world of violence, anger and mind games.

Things settled a little over the week, however I found it hard to stay focused at my job. I was organising funerals for people who had committed suicide and at the same time facing the very real threat of this happening in my own home. I sat at my desk and reflected on how hard I had worked to get into the funeral industry. Taking time off after only three weeks would look really bad and if I left the job I may never ever get another opportunity like it. I would have no money if I left the job, however if I stayed I could lose my son. I weighed up the options and chose to resign from my dream job to work with my son through this horrible time.

In doing this, I acknowledged my fears of 'never having another opportunity' and 'having no money', then took action to do what needed to be done.

Our days were spent with counsellors, talking, talking, and talking. I am not one to sit still so I asked my friend Dave if I could keep myself busy turning his little weekend sign-making hobby into a fully functioning business. I had no sales experience, no marketing experience and no income, but this project allowed me the flexibility to be there for my son and also keep my brain working. I am really not a stay-at-home kind of person. Josh came with me to the office a couple of days a week, and he spent a couple of days a week at school. We continued alternating days like this until he felt able to return to fulltime schooling.

On my first day of work I unfolded a green camping table and a crappy little chair in the tiny little dingy office. I pulled out the yellow pages and phoned anyone and everyone, having no idea about target markets. Then I knocked on anyone and everyone's doors asking for a sale. I was quite surprised when I actually started to make some sales.

The next hurdle was that I lived quite a distance from the office. As I was receiving no income from this job, I really had to think of ways to make it easier to get to work. One day I came home and told Dave, who by this stage was my partner, that we were moving house. I had signed a lease on a place an hour away from where we were, but much closer to the office. We had five days to move. I had been living in the same area for fifteen years so it was a big step to move away, but once again I acknowledged my fear, made a plan and got on with it.

We enrolled the kids in their new school but Josh found it hard to be separated from my Dad, to whom he was extremely close. He started high school but got caught up with the wrong crowd and really started to get out of control. After two years we finally made the difficult decision for Josh to move in with his grandfather.

It was incredibly difficult for me to let Josh go, and at the beginning I spent every evening in tears. Luckily I found out about the Tough Love concept and started using their techniques. I came to realise that I couldn't control Josh. The only person I could control was myself. This helped me to change the way I was approaching my relationship with my son, and I began to focus on talking positively with him rather than always nagging him to come back home. I worked with his school and with my Dad, arranging a counsellor for Josh as well as getting him into the Reach program. This support is still in place for Josh, and we now have a close and positive relationship and are in touch every day.

Had I not faced my fear of the unknown and moved through it, I would probably still be stuck where I was, and would never have had the opportunity to help myself and my children with our issues. I thank myself everyday for being that strong woman who faced her fears and just did what needed to be done.

Do you ever look back to when you were younger and remember that you had a dream of being something? Do you look back with regret at not fulfilling that dream? Do you continue to do what you are doing because it is safe and comfortable? Do you question why you never achieved the dreams you had all those years ago?

Perhaps what has been holding you back all those years is FEAR.

There are so many fears that can hold us back. The most important task to work on is to identify which fear you are being affected by, so you can deal with it. Do you have a fear of:

- Poverty

- Failure

- Success

- Public speaking

- Ending a relationship

- Getting out of your comfort zone

- Being judged

- Changing jobs

- Being alone

- Making decisions?

To assist you in your discovery, I would like to share a great exercise I learnt while completing the FIRE UP Coach Training Program.

Ask yourself these questions, and write the first answer that comes into your head:

When I imagine my dream goal, what is the negative voice in my head saying? eg. 'I'm just not smart enough to do that', or 'There are so many other smarter people than me'

_____

_____

When I hear that negative voice, what are my thoughts? e.g. 'I'll just accept I'm not smart enough and settle where I am', or 'I am comfortable where I am and after all, this job pays the bills'

_____

_____

I now realise that the fear that is holding me back is:

_____

_____

GREAT WORK!! You have now identified your fear and can begin to move past it.

To get a glimpse of how much this can affect your future, complete this exercise:

1. Imagine yourself five years from now. Sit quietly and really imagine yourself five years older. You are living all your dreams, passions and desires. Every dream you had years ago has actually happened and you are doing what you dreamt you would be doing. You have everything you desire. You are living your passion and purpose. Imagine what a day in your dream life is like. Imagine what you would do with your time, how you would feel, the contentment and happiness. Take note of the sensations, thoughts and actions you have in this image.

---

2. When you have explored how it would feel to be this 'future you', happy and fulfilled, select one area of your life you would really like to change. This might be your career, family relationships, personal relationships, health, looks, finances etc. Now that you are five years older and are living your dream life, how do you rate your level of satisfaction in this part of your life, on a scale of 1 to 10?

---

3. Look back five years to where you are today. How do you rate your level of satisfaction on a scale of 1 to 10 right now in this same part of your life?

_____

_____

4. So what changed? What thoughts and actions did you take in those five years to help you get to your new level of satisfaction? Ask your future self 'What is it I need from a friend/coach/mentor right now, to make this happen?'

_____

_____

5. If you hadn't taken those positive actions, how would your life look? Once, again, imagine yourself five years older; however this time you are still just getting by, doing a job you dislike to pay the bills. You have not achieved your dream life and in fact are fairly miserable. Imagine what you would do all day in your work, feel the disappointment and frustration.

_____

_____

6. Ask yourself 'What can I do differently today that will ensure I get the life I want?' Make a plan of five things you can do today to get the ball rolling.

_____

_____

7. Make it a habit to return to your dream life each and every day. While you are driving, before you go to sleep, when you wake up, when you are in the shower, any time is a good time to imagine you are living your dream life.

Thinking Outside The Square

Most people in society think very similar thoughts when trying to achieve success. This ultimately leads you to the same results as most people get, which is why so few people actually achieve great success.

The most successful people are the ones who think outside the square. Successful entrepreneurs see things differently to most people, and find ways to achieve their goals that others did not consider.

My ability to think outside the square probably grew from my natural survival instinct. When you come from an upbringing where you must find your own answers and solutions to your problems, it becomes a habit to think of different ways something can be achieved. I didn't want to do what everyone else was doing because I wanted superb results. To get superb results I had to think differently to everyone else.

This doesn't necessarily mean you need to do something no-one has ever done before, only that you need to be prepared to do it differently to the way you have always done it before.

One day I was having my nails done, and there was no-one in the salon but myself and the business owner. As she worked on my nails, the owner and I talked about her business and as usual I was asking lots of questions. She began to open up to me, telling me how the business was losing money and she didn't know what to do next. She was feeling depressed and it was affecting her relationship with her husband. She had tears in her eyes as she told me how her life was spiralling out of control. She had reached rock bottom and couldn't see a way out.

I asked 'How do you prospect for clients?' 'How do you encourage your customers to come back as repeat clients?' 'What marketing plan do you have?' I could not believe my ears when she had no answer to these three basic questions. I could not understand how she could be in business with no knowledge of these important topics. I was looking at her business differently to the way she was.

I felt so sorry for this lady that I offered to send her my marketing plan, prospect information and other business information to help her grow her business. She politely accepted my offer but I could see she wasn't very enthusiastic. Nevertheless I went home and emailed her the information.

Two weeks later I was back at the nail salon to have my nails refilled. I was amazed at the difference in this lady. She was smiling and full of energy. There was even a queue of customers waiting to get their nails done! Finally it was my turn, and she rushed over to give me a big hug. 'Thank you, thank you', she said 'Stacey you have no idea of how much your information has helped me'. She went on to tell me she had not realised the impact the information would have on her business. She had never thought of doing a marketing plan, and had no idea she could just pick up the phone and ask her customers if they needed their nails done. In two weeks her business had picked up, she was feeling so much more positive and she and her partner were in love again.

On my way home it hit me how looking at things differently, thinking outside the square, can totally change your outcome. As I have helped people with this over the years, it has proved time and time again to be a tremendous stepping stone on the journey to living their dreams.

Next time you come across a challenging problem, write down ten different ways you can come up with an answer. Starting from a place where you can't see a solution, you will soon be overwhelmed by all the choices you have to take action! Stop thinking like everyone else and start thinking for yourself and taking action.

Become the Person You Would Put on a Pedestal

I have attended countless workshops and seminars and bought so many books hoping for an answer. It took me a long time to realise the answers I was searching for were often in fact right inside me.

When I first started working in our business Signs 'n' Banners, it was run from a tiny office with only a small printer, my laptop, a folding camping table for a desk, and a second hand chair. I had no business, sales or marketing experience whatsoever.

On my first day there I got out the yellow pages, picked a group of businesses and started to phone each one looking for business. I did this day in day out until my list became quite large. Then I started to visit my clients and we would sit and talk, not only about my business, but about our real lives. Sometimes clients would call me up to have a chat, nothing else.

Although I didn't know anything about creative marketing at this point, I had noticed that people were quite intrigued by my personal journey. I started to think about creating a newsletter to email to my clients, called Stacey's Journey. This would save me time talking to each client and also let them know that I was a real person.

I didn't mention this to my partner or staff as I thought they would say it was a silly idea. But the feedback I got from clients was amazing. They would even forward on my newsletter to their friends to tell others about me and my business. My list grew at such fantastic rate I kept going until we grew out of that little office and into a factory.

As we grew, we decided to hire a business coach to help us with our systems and procedures. I stopped my unorthodox marketing tactics as I thought I should listen to the experts, the people I put on a pedestal. I thought our business coach might think my ideas were stupid and I was too embarrassed to show him what I was up to. So for three months I stopped doing my silly Stacey's Journey marketing and searched high and low for the real answer to marketing. I bought books, attended workshops and spoke to many successful business owners. My sales slowly went down and I was becoming drained, then one day after attending another workshop I had a huge BFO or Blinding Flash of the Obvious. The facilitator of the workshop, whom I had put on a pedestal, was recommending exactly what I had been doing all along. After that weekend I went back to what I was originally doing with my marketing, and our sales began to climb once again.

I'm sure you have come across similar situations when you have found the answers within yourself. We often look to others and even spend money on finding an answer when in fact it is already inside us if we dig deep.

Now each time I come across an obstacle I think I will need to pay others to solve, I first do a little exercise to make sure I don't have the answer within me. I know this will work for you too.

When you come across an obstacle:

1. Go to a quiet place with a pen and paper

2. Think back to a time in which you came across something similar and had the answer. Write down what you did

3. Write down some possible solutions to your current challenge, whether they seem feasible or not

4. Keep going until you find the answer within

5. If you still cannot find it, you'll know that the time to pay for guidance has come.

Women Wearing Masks

Women are complicated creatures. What you see is not always what you get. Lacking in good female role models when I was growing up, I felt intimidated by successful women and their seemingly perfect lives. Now I understand that most women wear masks to cover their issues and challenges. They only show the world the face they want people to see.

Like many young Mums I've always felt that older women had everything sorted out in their lives and looked down their nose at me. Thinking like this only lowered my self esteem further, until I 'got' the illusion. They were wearing masks. What an eye opener it was to realise that these women had their own issues to deal with, just like I did.

One of the mothers at my kids' school always made me feel envious. She was beautiful, had a lovely figure, gorgeous clothes, a husband, nice house, and car. I wondered what it would be like to live her life just for a day.

One afternoon I picked my kids up from school after a gruelling day in the family court. We walked over to the shops and saw this beautiful woman with her two children. My son ran over to say hello to her son and the woman and I started talking. I was feeling really down about what had happened in court and couldn't help sharing it with her, breaking down in tears right in front of her.

I couldn't believe my ears when she started to tell me about her divorce from her ex husband, the court fight, battles with her children, and challenges with her ex husband. Here was this woman I had looked up to telling me all these sad stories about her life.

She invited my son over to play that afternoon for the first time, and later on I went to pick him up. I found her enormous beautiful house and knocked on her door. She came out saying 'I'll shut the door because my grumpy partner will get angry if we talk too loud'. Wow, she was under the thumb, just like me. She told me that she wasn't married to her new partner, and he was not the father of her children. He owned the house, while she was struggling to afford the repayments on her fabulous car. The list of problems she was facing went on, and I didn't want to pity her but realised she had been wearing a mask all along.

I met other women like this and found that because I am so honest and direct about my life, this encourages them to open up also. Again and again I met women whose lives I envied, only to find out that they were not as perfect as they first appeared.

Slowly I learned to stop feeling envious of others and lived true to myself. I promised myself I would never ever wear a mask and pretend everything was ok. I made a pact with myself that if I needed help and support I would ask for it. I did not want my life crumbling slowly behind closed doors. I wanted my kids to learn to live a real, authentic life and to be true to themselves.

Years later, I was sitting outside the school waiting for my son. When the bell went he came running over to my car to ask if his friend could come over to play. He pointed out his friend's Mum and we introduced ourselves.

She was worried about how her son would behave at my home and asked me to call her if there were any problems. I reassured her by saying that my son had behaviour issues also, and went on to tell her about the trauma he had experienced in the violent relationship and the effect this had had on him. She opened up then and said that her son had wanted to play with mine before, but she had seen my great car and nice clothes and thought that my life looked so perfect that she was too shy to speak to me. I told her that I didn't wear a mask. What you see is what you get.

Comparing yourself to others doesn't help anyone. It just encourages all of us to continue to wear our masks for fear people will see the truth. Living in your own truth encourages those around you to do the same, and opens the door to better relationships with other women.

Life Without Mother

*H*aving a mother close by as you are growing up seems to be taken for granted by most people. But for people who haven't experienced that unconditional love and support, it is shown for the incredible gift it really is.

Sometimes I look at my children and think how lucky they are to have someone to wash their clothes, make their beds, cook them dinner, make their school lunches and drive them here there and everywhere. I also watch the whinging, the arguments, and their declarations of how they wish they had a different Mum, and realise they have no idea how lucky they are.

Being a Mum isn't just about cooking, cleaning and helping with homework. It's also about cuddling, caressing, spending quality time and being a role model for your children's future. Not having experienced this in your life can leave big gaps in your understanding of relationships and family life.

Some women lose their Mums through illness or a tragic accident. They may have memories of their Mum helping them with their hair, learning to read and nurturing them up until their Mum's passing.

Other women have no happy memories to look back on. If your mother dies or leaves when you are still a baby, you may be left with your father or other relatives, and never experience what a mother brings to a child's life. If you are lucky enough to have a great stepmum, grandma or aunty this can ease the pain, but if your mother leaves there will probably still be abandonment issues to deal with.

Mothers leave their babies for many reasons, such as:

- Drugs and alcohol problems

- Domestic violence

- Mental illness

- Another man enters their life

- They just can't cope with having children

How does this impact on you?

It is important for a baby's development to have a nurturing mother to protect, cuddle, and make you feel secure. As you grow older, Mums teach you to cook, show you how to do makeup and talk about girly things such as periods, sex and boys.

If you have been brought up without a Mum you may be feeling:

- Unwanted and unloved

- Envious of other girls who have a Mum

- Blaming yourself that your Mum left

- Unsure how to be a Mum yourself

- Not sure how to socialise with women

- Lacking understanding of women

- Looking for a mother role model

You can't do much about the choices your Mum made, but you can decide to manage your issues and move forward to become a great Mum yourself. You don't have to let this affect your whole life; you can do something about it.

The majority of women who have been raised without their Mums have abandonment issues. You may have effects such as:

- Not trusting anyone

- Becoming very clingy to your partner

- Being extremely jealous

- Having anger issues

Not trusting or respecting women

You may find yourself questioning the motives of other women. I didn't trust women at all and couldn't understand why they would try to help me by asking me to come to women's groups etc. One lady tried and tried but I just would not let her in to my life and was so rude to her that eventually she gave up. When she gave up on me I said to myself 'I knew she would do that'. It was like a game I played, to see how far I could push someone before they gave up on me. When they left I could blame them for what happened and move on to the next one. I had no concept of the hurt I caused, and it took me many years to understand and respect women.

Eventually I worked in an office full of women and had a chance to see that we actually had many of the same issues, challenges and ways of thinking. For the first time in my life I actually enjoyed being surrounded by women. I began to realise that women want to support each other, but it was a two-way street. I had to change my behaviour so that other women could trust me and get close to me, then I could trust them and be close to them.

Here are some small steps you can implement immediately to start trusting and respecting women.

- Talk to women; make it a goal to talk to a woman you admire but feel unworthy to talk to
- Keep your conversations positive
- Take notice of the way you speak about women, both negative and positive
- Be aware of the way in which you criticise women
- Talk openly about your issues. You will find that women usually understand how you feel and will be happy to share
- Don't bitch about women behind their backs
- Always make it a habit to only focus on the good traits of any woman
- Allow women into your life. If you close up, women will not trust you, so open up and be real. This allows them to open up also and you can begin to develop a relationship

Creating Healthy Relationships

No matter what your upbringing, we all bring issues into our personal relationships. These can be because of difficult upbringings, violent past relationships or the various scars and fears we pick up on our way through life. I have spent some time focusing on how I act in a relationship and have pinpointed a few common behaviours that many of us demonstrate.

Identifying these issues and working through them can leave you free to experience the high quality of relationships you have been looking for.

In order to be in the perfect relationship we must behave like the perfect partner, so be honest as you read, and look for behaviours you are ready and willing to let go of to allow the perfect relationship into your life.

Clinginess

When I was in my younger relationship I became so clingy to my boyfriend that I forgot all my friends and spent all my time alone with him. I was so fearful of him leaving me that I felt the need to be with him at all times. I worried that if I went out, he would meet someone else. It was a terrible way of living. We didn't have hobbies or go out without each other, and argued constantly as we tried to control each other.

Eventually I realised that this clinginess only stunted our growth as people. Holding on so tight eventually causes the other person to become frustrated and want to get away from you, which is exactly what you were trying to avoid.

Now, whenever I feel that need to hold on tight, I talk myself through it. To do this, focus on your thoughts and feelings when you are feeling clingy. Ask yourself these questions:

- What is my stomach feeling?

- What are my thoughts saying?

- What am I fearful of happening?

- Why am I feeling unloved by my partner?

- What can I do to feel loved by myself?

- When my partner wishes to do something by himself, what can I do for myself that would make me feel special and loved by myself?

- If I am left at home with the children, what can we do together to keep my mind from wanting my partner?

It's absolutely healthy for you and your partner to do things you love on your own. Continue your friendships outside the relationship and ensure your partner does also. Try taking one night a week each to follow your own hobbies and interests. Support each other by looking after the children while the other goes out.

When your partner arrives home, avoid questioning him about where he has been. This is hard at first but try to just ask him how his time was. Make it a positive conversation.

While your partner is out, keep your mind busy by playing and having fun with your children. Everyone will benefit from having a positive family experience, and you will be amazed at how quickly things change in your family. Your self esteem rises, your partner loves coming home to you, and best of all your kids have happy parents.

Jealousy

When I was living in a bad relationship, my partner was extremely jealous and didn't like me wearing short skirts, or talking or even looking at other men. It got to the point that I couldn't have any friends because he would become so jealous. My self esteem started to get lower and lower, and I had no self belief.

I thought so little of myself that I began to panic that he would leave me. I started to use the same jealous behaviour he did, and would accuse him of not loving me if I saw him looking at another woman. Every day while he was at work, I would be worrying who he was talking to and what he was doing. Our jealousy became so bad that we started to physically hurt each other in our jealous rages.

When I finally left this relationship and worked on myself I learnt why I was feeling jealous, it was because of my low self esteem. Finally after many years I started to love who I was and stopped comparing myself to other girls. It took a lot of work to build my self esteem and feel confident, but it was worth it. I was able to start a new relationship without the jealousy taking over.

There are two kind of jealousy:

Healthy Jealousy

- Feeling annoyed when your partner is flirting with someone
- Feeling upset about your partner going out to the movies with someone and then a dinner afterwards

Unhealthy Jealousy

- Obsessively looking around for people your partner might be attracted to whenever you go out
- Watching your partner to see what he is looking at
- Questioning your partner's every move
- Getting angry and abusive when an attractive person comes on the TV
- Becoming angry if your partner's ex is mentioned

If you have unhealthy jealousy in your relationship, you will need to start working on your own self esteem.

Start to notice what it is you are jealous of in other women. If it is what they are wearing, consider whether you might like to try those styles yourself. If they seem to be leading exciting lives, have a look at what you might like to do in your own life.

Turn the jealousy into admiration. When you are talking to someone who you would feel jealous of, compliment her on her great hairdo or nice dress. Practice turning the jealousy into something positive. This will make both you and her feel better about yourselves.

Anger

If you were bought up in an abusive or neglectful environment, you may have learned to express your feelings using anger. This is a learned behaviour – when you are frightened or worried about something, it comes out as anger at other people.

There are times when anger is appropriate, but if you recognise these behaviours your anger may be unhealthy:

- You are frequently having arguments with neighbours, friends, relatives, strangers etc

- You get angry over small things

- You have lost a job because of your anger

- Your family is scared when you become angry

- Your partner and children walk around on egg shells

- You yell, swear, hit and kick walls

- You physically hit out at your partner, children or animals

Changing unhealthy anger habits takes a lot of commitment, especially if you have been this way for a long time. With practice, you can control your emotions rather than have them control you.

- Start to recognize your feelings and thoughts when you can feel yourself getting angry. How does your stomach feel? Are you sweating? What thoughts are running through your head?

- Tell the people you are with that you need some clear thinking space and take yourself away from the situation. Go and sit outside for 10 minutes.

- Explain to your partner that you are working on your anger and ask him to support you

- Be aware when you are trying to control the people around you

- Ask for help if you need it, and allow others to help you

- Take time out each week to refresh yourself

- If a car pulls out in front of you, don't yell and toot the horn. Be aware of your feelings and thoughts and then think of a positive thought. Breathe

- If you feel your partner is not helping out enough around the house, make a time to sit together and talk it through. You are more likely to get him to help if you talk to him with respect

- Accept that it will take time for you to stop becoming angry constantly, so be prepared to stick it out.

Whatever has happened in your upbringing and through your life has already happened. You can't change it now. However you can change the way you behave from now on. There is no point having your past ruin the life you have in front of you.

You do have the power to change your own life and you are responsible for the person you are now. You owe it to your children to be a good role model and give them the best possible chance of a happy childhood. Model the skills you would like them to take into their lives with them.

Tackling the Green Eyed Monster

I really can't see the point in getting jealous of other people's success. I go out of my way to look for successful people so I can learn from them. I look at their traits and work on growing these in myself.

As a young girl we always had the worst house in the street, a housing commission house. We would sometimes have a family car if Dad picked up a bargain for around $150. You can imagine the quality of these cars; they were never registered and Dad would just drive them till they blew up. Then we would have no car for another couple of years until he found another $150 bargain.

When I was thirteen I visited my boyfriend's house and couldn't believe my eyes. Not only did his parents own a house but they also owned not one but two cars. I remember questioning his Mum to try to find out how they managed to pay for these things. This is where I first learned the lesson that if you want something enough, it is only YOU that is stopping you from having it.

I decided to learn what I could from these people, so at sixteen, after I had my first baby, I told my boyfriend's parents that I really wanted to get a car by the time I turned eighteen. I asked for their advice on how I could do it and they told me that I would need to save half my wage from working as a waitress. As an incentive, they said that if I could do this they would buy the car and fix it up for me. My boyfriend's Dad was a panel beater. I worked really hard and managed to save half the money and so by the time I turned eighteen I owned my first car.

I couldn't quite believe that after so many years of living without a car, I actually owned one of my own. It was only a VB Commodore but I loved it and was so proud of myself for making my dream come true. At this point in my life the quality of my friends was very low and none of them had a job, let alone own a car. I was the only one working and I was also the only one with a child. I had big dreams and desires, while they spent their days smoking pot and complaining about how crap their lives were.

Of course now the green eyed monster started to appear. Someone was obviously jealous of my first signs of success, and my car was constantly keyed down the side, and had the panels kicked in. My boyfriend had also managed to save for a car and his car was stolen from our driveway and torched. I know it was the people we were hanging out with back then; remember the quality of your friends determine the quality of who you become!!

Of course soon my little old VB started to die a slow death and with no heating, the kids and I would have to get dressed in a beanie, scarf, and gloves to go in the car. I made a commitment to my kids that I would buy a new car once I had saved enough money.

I was working fulltime as an Accountant's Assistant and completing my Certificates in Business Management when I was finally able to buy a brand new VX Commodore, complete with air conditioning and heating. I had worked my butt off for this for many years and couldn't wait to visit my friends and show them how I was living my dreams and moving forward in a big way.

I tooted my horn out the front of their house in excitement, imagining they would come running out wanting to go for a spin. How wrong I was. Not only did they not want to look at my new car but they told me I was full of myself. One friend even wrote me a letter to say that just because I had a full time job, a nice house and a car did not mean I was the best.

I had thought after growing up with so little that it was natural for me to get excited when I created success in my life. I learned another hard lesson – not to get too excited in front of others when you purchase something you have dreamed of, such as a car, house or clothes.

That lesson even stays with me today. When my partner came home last year with a new X5 BMW, I told him not to show anyone or tell anyone it was ours. Even when I bought my dream home I was careful who I mentioned it to. I have worked very hard to create a comfortable life; it has not been handed to me on a platter by any means.

Dealing with the jealousy of those around me was a real struggle for me, and as my life started to move forward I became scared that my success would mean I would lose the people close to me. I began to turn down business opportunities and media interviews through fear that any future success would mean I would lose my family and friends.

In 2009 my son and I attended a Money and You seminar and one of the topics was Fear of Success. Boy did I relate to that one! That weekend I realised that I had two choices. I could pursue my dreams and goals and risk losing family and friends, or I could stay where I was and keep my negative friends and family around me. I did a lot of crying that weekend but realised I had a mission to accomplish, to inspire and empower women and men to become what they dream of. I could not allow other people's jealousy to get in the way of my growth, and had to live by my motto, 'If you are powered by passion, all things are possible'.

Since then I have allowed so much more into my life, taking up challenges and opportunities I would have turned down in the past. Yes, it has cost me some family and friends. I have lost three people who were very close to me since that weekend, and this saddens me. I also have to deal with criticism about the way I do things. Some women are resentful that I have a nanny, and I know I am very lucky to have Dave's Mum look after my two babies every day for nine months of the year. However I didn't have this kind of support with my three older kids, and still managed to achieve great things.

If you are feeling a little jealous of someone else's success, try not to fall into the habit of saying nasty things about them. Look at what it is they have that you are jealous of and then use it as an example to set about creating your very own success. Most successful people work very hard at what they do, and you can use their experiences to inspire your own success. You might find the key to allow you to jump on board as an entrepreneur. It's a fun ride, draining, exciting, frustrating, but so worth it!

Stay focused on YOU and only YOU. Jealousy will stunt your growth. If you are finding yourself losing some of the people around you as you move forward, let go with love and stay focused on your vision.

Mentors

I can not emphasise enough the importance of having people around you who believe in you. I have had many people tell me that I dream too big and I should get back to reality. That's ok, I just move away from them and find people who can help me get to the next level on my journey. I love to have people around me who had a big dream and made it happen. I only choose people I know have made their own dreams a reality. I will never ever stop asking people for advice and if someone is already doing something I want to do, I never ever hesitate to contact that person, no matter who they are. You will be amazed at how many people are actually willing to spend time sharing their wisdom and helping you reach your goals.

It is important to gather as much advice as you can, but you must ultimately do what feels right for you. I have had the most amazing feedback but I only take advice on board if I feel it is right in my gut. If my gut tells me it's not right, then I am grateful for the advice and file it away.

I am so grateful to all the people who have supported me on my journey. It does not take one single person to become a success; it takes a team of people who share your vision. Success happens when you find the right people who share your values. All successful people have a team around them. It's up to you to find the people who will support your dreams and visions.

You've got to back yourself and trust your own decisions.
Remember, the most expensive advice is
free advice from a poor person

Brad Sugars

Family

Although I didn't have a very stable background and very little contact with my Mum, my Dad was always a great mentor to me. Dad was passionate about ensuring that his children had lots of freedom and fun and didn't experience any abuse. What ended up happening was that he lived his childhood again alongside his own children, and often we would have to act like parents to him. We had very little in the way of rules and boundaries, and when Dad did try to put his foot down I would cry and beg until he gave in. I found it very difficult to settle in to the structure of school or any kind of authority really, but did grow up to be a very strong-minded girl.

Because Dad encouraged me to experience so many different things with no fear, I never really learned to be fearful. He always gave me the freedom to be me and encouraged me in whatever I chose to do. All around me were teachers, friends' parents, and people from church telling me how naughty I was, however Dad always stood by me. When I had my first child so young he was the only one who didn't tell me I had ruined my life. Others cringed at his parenting skills, and I must say sometimes I look back and can't believe the stuff I was allowed to do, however it has made me the woman I am today.

Respect is a big focus for Dad, and it must have been hard for him to watch me being so disrespectful to those around me. Eventually I learned he was right, and I now have developed a genuine respect for myself and others.

Dad passed on his greatest passion to me also. Although he didn't have a lot of money, he was always the first to reach out a helping hand to those in need. Helping others is what keeps him ignited and on fire. I know I picked up the same trait from Dad, and it has been such a wonderful gift. We both get our kicks from seeing others flourish and phone each other every week to report in on what we have done to help someone that week.

As you can see, finding mentors in your family is not only for those with 'white picket fence' upbringings. You might find that you have different lessons to learn from different members of your family, or you could have one person who really stands out who is prepared to take you under their wing.

Surrogate family

Having an unusual childhood meant that there wasn't a big pool of mentors in my family to draw from. So I borrowed someone else's family!

Josh and Tahlia's father introduced me to his family and what an eye-opener that was. When I visited their home I discovered that both the parents had jobs, they owned a house and not one but two cars. The house was always spotlessly clean and when the parents came home from work they said hello to each other.

I stayed at their house as often as I could as I loved the cleanliness, the happiness, and the closeness. I was amazed that each night we would have dinner at the same time and would get the best lunches to take to school the next day. I actually questioned my boyfriend as to why they had dinner every single night. I couldn't quite comprehend how all this was possible, but I loved my first experience of being in a functional family.

I am so grateful for everything they taught me, such as how to find a job and how to save up for my first car. They helped me get my learner's permit and then encouraged me to get my P-plates. In the week I turned eighteen I passed my driving test with flying colours, and had my own car to drive.

I needed a role model for being in a successful family, and even though I couldn't find this in my own family, I found a family that could help me.

The lessons I learned from this family have helped me enormously through my life. I saved for my dream home and still keep the house spotlessly clean. And every night we eat dinner at the same time.

Perhaps you have friends who have the kind of family you wish you had. Spending time with these people can give you amazing insights into how to be a part of a successful family, and you can pick up skills to take back home.

Partner

I am lucky enough to have found in my fiancé Dave a true example of how a real man should treat their partner. Dave has taught me so much about myself. He has allowed me to shine and be the real me. He allows me to make my dreams happen. When I want to express love he allows it, when I want to express anger he allows it and when I want to express fear he allows it. Dave never puts me down, he just stays out of my way and supports me to be me. He knows I have big dreams and always supports me to reach them. I am allowed to have my own thoughts, take my own actions and be who I want to be. We are not just one in the relationship; we are two people who are in love. We both respect each other's dreams, wants and desires.

When we discussed having children together, I was really clear that I still wanted to pursue my dreams and goals. Dave promised me he would support me and be there to help me raise our children, and has certainly kept to his word. We share the tasks evenly – if I cook he baths the kids, if he cleans I bath the kids, we both take it in turns to get up to feed the babies at night. We are a great team; we don't fight, we don't put each other down and we laugh a lot.

Dave saw something in me that I knew I had but it needed work to bring it out. With his love and support my fire burned brighter and I took my dreams to the next level. Having Dave's love and support has also allowed me to become the Mum I always knew I could be. I am free to love my kids the way I always dreamt was possible and for that I truly am living my dreams.

Not everyone's partner is as supportive as mine, but most have some good qualities. Take some time to think about how your partner supports you, even in the smallest of ways, by paying you compliments or helping out with the cooking occasionally. Let them know how grateful you are for their support – this is the surest way to encourage them to do more of the same!

Remember the BE-DO-HAVE rule. To have the perfect relationship you must act like the kind of person who would be in that perfect relationship. You must BE that person, and DO what they would do in order to HAVE what they have. If you act with your highest integrity in your relationship, it will encourage your partner to do the same and you will both move closer to your goal.

Friends

You become the kind of person you spend time with. When I was younger I hung around with a lot of people who didn't have jobs and liked to sit around smoking pot and complaining about how hard life was. Once I embarked on my mission to live my dream life, I decided to only have positive friends. I was lonely for quite a while, but then things began to change.

Chrissy was the first friend I made when I set a goal to only allow positive people into my life. I met her at a business networking event and she is like the Mum I never had. Chrissy is older than me but we talk the same language. We feed off each other's achievements, and meet up every week to walk together and talk about all the amazing things that have happened in the few days since we saw each other last. I have never heard a negative word come out of Chrissy's mouth. She believes in me and knows I will succeed.

When Chrissy says she will do something she will do it. If we make plans together I know she will follow through, which I find is surprisingly rare in a friend. She is quite a spiritual person and has helped me work on that side of my life. Chrissy is also an amazing Mum to her two children and has given me some valuable parenting tools. She has helped me through issues with my children and I always find her advice spot on target.

When you are on a mission to reach your dreams, friends like this are vital. It is really important to find someone to share your excitement with and support each other through the challenges. Seek out positive, forward thinking people and nurture these friendships.

The boss

I worked full time for Cliff for nearly four years and we clicked from the first day. He wasn't looking for staff when I knocked on his door but he was impressed by my initiative in asking him for work and so he took me on anyway. Every morning, Cliff would greet me with 'Good morning my little chickadee'. When I told him my dreams, he believed I could achieve them. Cliff chose tasks for me that he knew would develop my skills and push me to show leadership. Completing each task successfully lifted my self esteem and I wasn't afraid to ask questions. Cliff always took the time to explain something I didn't understand and never got angry.

Cliff treated me like a lady and in fact was the first man to show me how a gentleman behaved. He showed me a world where I was treated with respect. At first it seemed very strange and I thought he lived on another planet, however now I expect and deserve to be treated this way by everyone I meet. He did plan to teach me to speak with a plum in my mouth, but I guess I was not born to be that much of a lady!

Even the most mundane of jobs can offer mentoring opportunities. Wonderful people work in all kinds of industries, people who will take the time to help you learn and grow, and support you in your goals. If you find yourself working in an organisation with a boss like this, think yourself lucky and learn what you can while you are there!

Counsellors

I call Donna my angel sent from above. She is my shining star. I was court-ordered to attend her sessions and am so glad I was given this opportunity. Donna had faith in me when no one else did. She knew just as strongly as I did that I would succeed with my dream and was there for me every step of the way. I called her at all hours and no matter what time it was, she would comfort me. She told me that what I was experiencing was totally normal and that I would get through it. She also told me that I was a good Mum at a time when I had been hearing only the opposite. Donna nurtured my self development and having her as my counsellor absolutely changed my life. I am so thankful that Donna came into my life when she did.

Counsellors specialise in a number of different areas. If you are struggling with one particular area of your life, whether it is parenting, relationships, career, abuse or something else, you will find a counsellor who can help you.

However there are more than qualifications to consider when choosing a counsellor. You may need to meet with a few different counsellors until you find one you click with. Look for a counsellor who makes you feel comfortable, who has a style of talking that you find easy to understand, and who you trust enough to be honest with. It sounds like a lot to find in one person, but they are certainly out there.

If you would like to contact Donna to discuss your counselling needs, you can get her on ws_dnn@yahoo.com.au or 0402 830691.

Professional training

I went along to the FIRE UP Coach Training Program to learn all I could about coaching and came out with a tremendous increase in confidence in my abilities. The sixteen-day course made me realise I could help so many thousands of women become what they dream of. Without Kathy McKenzie's belief in me to begin with, I would never have had the opportunity to truly get inside myself and realise I was an intelligent woman.

We never stop learning in our careers. There are always opportunities to go further and learn more about the way we do business. Continuous education keeps us at the front of the field, and keeps the fires of motivation burning. Take the opportunities that come along to find out how other people are doing things, and to be sure that you are always looking for different ways to reach your goal.

Business coaching

Our business Signs 'n' Banners had grown to such a level that I needed someone to look at the business from an outside perspective and advise us on where to go next. I wanted a coach who walked the talk and was a straight shooter. Someone who would not be soft on me, someone with a great deal of integrity and someone who would keep me accountable at all times. The minute I interviewed Jan Bidstrup, I knew I had found the right business coach; he had all these qualities and more.

Jan tells it like it is, and will not allow me to make excuses but always keeps me on track towards my goals. Not only has Jan been a great business coach but he has become a friend I can talk to about any subject. Each time I ring Jan with a dilemma in our business he makes time to talk through it with me. After these conversations I can see each challenge in a new positive light, and am reminded that not everything is how I perceive it to be.

I have another more informal business coach, Dominique Lyone from Complete Office Supplies. I met Dominique when my son and I attended the Money and You seminar Dominique facilitated. The seminar was an amazing experience for both my son and myself, and helped us to explore our own intelligence through a series of games designed to bring out the entrepreneur in each of us. During the seminar I heard how Dominique started a little business, overcame countless obstacles and eventually turned Complete Office Supplies into a multimillion dollar company. I wanted to be around this man to learn from him, so after the seminar I just walked up and asked him if he could be my business mentor. Kindly enough he took me up on this and we still keep in touch. Whenever I have a query he's at the end of the phone, another person to give me their personal perspective on my issue.

Sometimes it can be hard to justify spending money on a business when we are usually so focused on saving money. However business coaches can look at how your business is run with fresh eyes, and can see different ways of doing things. Often we can't see other ways to organise everything because we are so busy working on the day-to-day running of the business. The money spent on a business coach is usually recovered quickly, through more efficient processes. There are also incredible long-term benefits, as a coach will make you sit down and plan where you are trying to go with your business, and how to get there. Goals are always so much easier to reach with a clear plan in place.

Business peers

Andrew Smith of Dr Drip Plumbing is a male version of me. I was introduced to Andrew with the words 'Stacey, meet Andrew. You need to get to know him because he is a plumber'. Before I could stop it my big mouth blurted out the response 'Why would I need to get to know Andrew if he is just a plumber?' I could have curled up and died right then and there.

Luckily Andy gave me another chance and that night when we went out for dinner with a group of friends, I found out that he was not only a funny guy, he was a seriously successful business man. We had so much in common in our passions for business and our families that I was drawn to him. Andy was easy to talk to about business situations I found myself in, as he had experienced many of the same issues in his own business. It was great to hear him talk about how he got through each challenge.

I found another great friend in Wendy Bentley of Think For Fitness. I attended an event where Wendy was speaking about how she had written, edited and published her own book in ten days. She was a true leader and we hit it off straight away. Wendy totally 'gets' me and can see my strengths through my frustrations. She has helped me enormously with my branding and I can see us doing amazing things together.

Having friends in business who understand what you are going through as you grow your own business is so valuable. Business peers can come from the strangest of places. Finding people you connect with who have a common passion for business can be a great support. You will often find that other business owners will have faced similar issues to those you are facing, and will understand the challenges you are dealing with.

Many areas have networking groups where you can meet other like-minded business owners. The people you meet might not necessarily be in the same type of business that you are, but sometimes it is more important that you share the same philosophies or outlooks with other entrepreneurs.

Specialised professional support

I had never written a book before and knew I would have a lot to learn. While I was still writing I was approached by three publishers, however after doing a lot of research I decided self publishing was the way to go. It was a steep learning curve to self publish my first book, so I sought out all the help I could find.

My editor Alex Mitchell of www.AuthorSupportServices.com came recommended by bestselling author Sandy Forster. I had interviewed four editors but something kept guiding me back to Alex. She was supportive from the very beginning, even before the contract was signed. I didn't know too much about writing a book, but every question I asked Alex she answered happily and knew what she was talking about. After a few months of interviewing other editors I knew Alex was the one for me. She has guided me through the whole process, helping me get everything in the right place and making sure my book was focused on my reader not just Stacey's story. Alex has contributed so much knowledge to my book that I have no idea how I would have done it without her. Originally I thought my editor would just edit my book and we would be done. No, no, Alex has helped me with the wording on my back cover, given me feedback on my chapters, and helped put together all those extra pages which need to be in a book.

I am so very happy with my decision to go with my gut, I felt from day one Alex was the editor for me. It can be so easy just to listen to everyone else's ideas and lose sight of your own self belief. The universe will send you the people you need when you need them, and it is important to train yourself to listen when your gut tells you it is the right time.

Rachael Bermingham was made famous through her series of 4 Ingredients cook books. I saw her speak at a business event on how she made her dreams happen and went from being thousands of dollars in debt to running a multimillion dollar business and becoming a self published bestselling author. Incredibly, nine weeks before I saw her speak she had given birth to twin boys. I was drawn to her passion, determination and excitement for life.

I just couldn't help myself, I contacted Rachael to ask for some advice on book publishing. She gave her valuable time to talk me through the processes and gave constructive criticism where she believed I needed more attention. Rachael even offered to distribute the book for me through Bermingham Books.To have this feedback from someone who knows what they are talking about is extremely important when you are trying to achieve something you don't know much about.

Dale Beaumont is another amazing bestselling author I managed to connect with. I first came across Dale years ago when I purchased some of his Secrets Exposed series of books. I was intrigued by his success at self publishing and wanted to see if he could help me. I managed to get in touch with Dale and although he has a very busy schedule he took his time to give me some useful tips and information on becoming a self published bestselling author.

Finding your mentors

It can be daunting to find the right people to give you advice and support. The trick is to recognise where you need help, and to recognise an expert when you see one. Everyone is an expert in something. The right mentor for you may not be the person with the most qualifications, it could be someone in your family who inspires you, or the boss at work who takes you under their wing.

Don't feel you need to rush out and find a mentor in every area of your life. Concentrate on what you need right now and see what resonates with you. The right person will often appear in your life at just the right moment if you have your eyes and ears open ready to learn and listen.

Instead of Following, Lead and Show Others the Way

As various challenges have come up in my life I have often felt confused, lost, frustrated, and desperate. To find a way forward I would look for leaders I could follow, people who had already succeeded and could show me the way.

I thought that to get ahead, I could just ask successful people how to do things or pay them to do it for me, hoping my answers would then magically appear and I would be on my way. I have found some great people and received some wonderful advice, but of course I kept finding that successful people had limited time to help me.

When I started to really focus on turning my life around, I became hungry for answers and advice from young Mums who had lived through similar experiences to mine and gone on to reach their goals. I googled successful young Mums, I went to the library to look for books on successful young Mums but could not find anything about young Mums who had lived through domestic violence, sexual abuse or a traumatic childhood and had managed to defy the odds. I was once again searching for a leader who I could learn from, who could hand me the answers I needed to move forward.

As I sat on the beach thinking about this problem, I was reminded of another time I had felt frustrated and confused trying to find answers. I had been trying to get work in the funeral industry and had been looking for people who could help me get my foot in the door. I read the Funeral Industry Association website every day, and even asked for advice from a funeral industry worker I had tracked down from an article written in a magazine. I felt that I was doing everything I could to get the advice I needed, but still nothing happened.

Then I decided to step up and take the lead. At nineteen years old, I walked into the local funeral company with my three year old and four month old in tow, and asked for a job. I told the owner that I had nowhere to live, two babies and a passion for the funeral industry. I asked him when I could start work. I think perhaps he thought I was crazy, as he told me to come back another time.

I went home and got out all the job adverts and position descriptions I had collected from the funeral industry. I used these to make up a pretend resume, showing all the experience and skills I would need to have in order to get the job I wanted. The next day I walked down to the funeral company without my children and asked the manager whether he would offer me a position if I had all the experience shown on the resume.

He said that yes, if I had all the experience and skills shown on the resume he would offer me a position. I set about taking action to acquire each of the skills listed, and even checked in with the manager every six months to show him what I had achieved. Eventually I had everything I needed and was offered a position.

Sitting on the beach that day, I realised I was in the same position again, looking to others for answers that were inside me. Once again in order for me to move forward I had to get out of my comfort zone and look at doing things a different way. In order for me to succeed, I had to become the leader I was searching for. Once I realised this, I knew what I needed to do. I stepped up and took the lead and things just fell into place. What a learning experience this journey has been for me.

I set about studying other successful leaders, leaders who came from great backgrounds as well as not so great backgrounds, women, men, all types of leaders. As I studied these leaders I began to realise that I had many of the same traits and characteristics they had. I didn't need to keep looking for that special leader for all the answers, I actually had the answers inside me all along. I became determined and committed to becoming a leader myself, and with this decision my confidence skyrocketed.

I realised that I could be a leader to other young Mums and show them that there was another way to live. When I was given the choice at the hospital that day to leave my violent partner or lose my children, I was forced to discover that there was another way to live. I had known other ways existed but I assumed that was just for lucky people. I didn't realise you could make those changes yourself. My mission was to inspire and empower other young Mums so they could also take charge of their lives.

I set about taking my learnings and teaching them to other young Mums at community houses. I put together a training course focusing on vision boards, to help these young women discover their passions and bring out the strengths they had within them.

I believed in my purpose so strongly that I knew I had to get my message out on a larger scale. I approached the project in the same way I would build a successful business. I had a website built and studied books on sales, marketing and public relations.

At the same time I implemented everything I learnt to grow our business Signs 'n' Banners. I took this business to a point where I could leave our employees to manage everything while I took two days a week off to focus on writing my book.

I looked at attending book publishing courses at a cost of thousands of dollars but again I decided to just read books, google for information and ask great leaders for advice. I made a decision, created a plan and worked hard. I learned all I could about writing a book, networked with highly successful publishers, had an incredible amount of self belief, took responsibility and continually visualised the end result. Most importantly I didn't waste time thinking too much about what needed to be done. I just got started and didn't stop until I finished.

If you have a passion and desire for something and are asking advice from lots of people, you will find a lot of different opinions on any subject. Some of it will be good advice, some won't. It is up to you to decide what is right for you and then to implement it. There is no point paying others to tell you how to do something, then sitting back and waiting for success to arrive. People who do this often end up complaining that they wasted their money on something that didn't work, when in fact they simply didn't take the action needed to create their success.

There are plenty of people out there waiting for others to take them to the top. If you keep searching and waiting for others to get you there, it will never ever happen. You must step up, take action and lead the way towards your own success. Once you take control of your destiny by becoming a leader, the right people will come to you to help you on your way.

Healthy Lifestyle — Make it a Habit

When you make the decision to get on the road to success, it is crucial for you to not only have a healthy mind but a healthy body also.

There is incredible power in balancing a healthy diet, exercising, socialising, having family time, sleeping well and drinking lots of water. You don't need to be an expert on health to know that keeping your body in good shape will help you achieve more every day. On the other side, if you drink, smoke, don't exercise and don't get enough sleep you will feel less motivated to achieve your goals.

I have studied many successful people and find that one thing most of them have in common is their emphasis on living a healthy lifestyle. This enables them to have energy; it helps keep their life in balance and keeps their vision clear.

I decided to take on this lesson and now find I can bounce out of bed every morning energised, motivated, goal driven and focused.

Food

I start my day with a fresh juice and eat six healthy meals a day. I am no expert in this field, but do know that once you start eating a healthy diet you will feel so much fresher.

An example of a healthy daily diet would be:

6am	Juice
7am	Muesli and yoghurt

10am	Yoghurt and almonds
Noon	Salad with either chicken or tuna. Throw in some baby spinach, tomatoes, cucumber, red onion, cos lettuce, and drizzle with balsamic vinegar
3pm	Crackers with avocado and tzatziki dip, or carrots and celery with hommus dip
6.30pm	Fish or steak with vegetables, or stir fried meat and vegetables

What does your daily food intake look like? Try writing down what you eat every day for a week. You will see the patterns in your eating emerge, and may find areas where you can improve the way you plan your meals.

Exercise

Exercise is critical to keeping a healthy body and positive mindset. You only need 45 minutes a day to make a difference. Try walking, running, squats, skipping, sit ups or, push ups, they are all free!

It's absolutely amazing how much fitter and motivated you will feel, just give it a go.

Water

Try to drink at least two and half litres of water a day. Yes you will be going to the toilet all day; yes at first it will be a struggle, but boy will you feel great!!

Some of the benefits of drinking water are:

• Water helps you lose weight by flushing out fat products

• Drinking water reduces hunger

• Being properly hydrated means you will experience fewer headaches

• Your brain is made up mostly of water, so the more water you drink the better you think. You will be more alert and able to concentrate better

- Your skin will glow, as water helps replenish skin tissue, moisturises your skin and increases its elasticity

- Drinking water reduces feelings of tiredness as it flushes toxins and waste from your body. Without enough water your heart needs to work harder to pump the oxygenated blood to your cells, which exhausts your vital organs and exhausts you.

On days I don't drink enough water, I feel fatigued, dehydrated and lacking in energy, so I know it is working for me.

YOU time

One of the main things that allows me to stay fit and healthy while running a business and raising my children is ME time. It can be one of the hardest commitments to squeeze into the day but makes all the difference. I make time to go shopping, visit a friend, walk on the beach with a friend, get a spray tan or sit on the beach and read, whatever makes me feel great.

I also support my partner to take time out for his hobbies and he supports me to schedule in my time. If I am feeling tired or stressed, he will take the children and I will go and do something that I know will make me feel positive. When I arrive back home I feel on fire again and ready for family time. For me to be a happy positive Mum, I need that time out to reenergise myself and refocus my thoughts, feelings and visions.

Unfortunately many people don't take time out for themselves, but it is vital to step away sometimes and recharge your batteries so you can stay full of energy. Make a commitment with your partner or a friend to support each other's time out; you never know what magic will be rekindled when you unwind a little!

Family time

How often do you sit together as a family and have a chat? Do you regularly ask each other how your day was and actually listen to the answer?

Our computer-based lives are making it increasingly difficult to spend family time together. At our home we have instigated a new activity. Once dinner is finished, the dishes have been cleaned and the house is tidy, we don't turn on the TV. We all sit together in the lounge room and just chill out together. Sometimes we watch the babies play or we all just sit and talk. It doesn't matter if my teenagers don't feel like talking some nights, what matters most is that we are all together in the same room.

Start a new habit to turn off the TV and spend family time talking or even walking together. It's amazing some of the topics that come up when there is time to just chat.

Sleep

I love sleep. A good night's sleep is what pumps me and makes me feel motivated. I jump out of bed full of energy and enthusiasm. I have to get up to feed my babies through the night so I need at least seven hours sleep each night to feel brilliant.

What are your sleeping habits like? Do you stay awake until midnight, wake up early and wonder why you just want to curl up and go back to sleep? Try going to bed at around 9pm and notice the difference. It might take a while to get used to going to bed earlier, but you will see a massive difference in your energy levels.

If you are on a journey towards living your dream life, I can't emphasise enough the importance of taking action and beginning today to live a healthy lifestyle. I can only give you the information; you will need to take charge to make this happen.

Characteristics and Traits of Highly Successful People

Why is it that we are all born with the same set of fingers, toes, eyes, ears and nose and yet some of us turn out to be rich people and some of us turn out to be poor people? Why are some of us successful and some unsuccessful?

Everybody has their own definition of success. Some people want to become millionaires, some billionaires. Some want fame and fortune, and others crave the time to be alone and at peace.

As I child I found it hard to watch the constant juggle my Dad and stepmum had, trying to keep up with the rent and bills. I watched them argue as they got so far behind in rent payments that we were in danger of losing the house. This constant underlying fear that we would have nowhere to live meant I have grown up acutely aware of how important it is to have a home where my kids could feel secure. It's no surprise then that my definition of success was to own my own home.

As I studied successful people, I looked closely at their traits and characteristics. I began to realise that successful people don't just do one or two things well, they do many things and they work on them daily. Success is not something you can achieve by going to a seminar or taking a magic pill. Success is hard work.

The good news is that you can learn to become successful and learn the traits that other successful people have learnt.

Have a dream or passion

All successful people have a passion and a purpose in life. Each action they take is designed to take them another step closer to fulfilling their passion and purpose. They know exactly where they are going and are always focused on the end result. Obstacles that appear don't stop them from their mission to do whatever it takes to pursue their vision.

Work to a plan

Successful people develop and implement a plan of action. They visualise the end result and work backwards. Without a plan, you cannot be sure that the action you are taking today will in fact lead you to the goal you have set for yourself. Create a plan of action and stick to it.

Never ever take no for an answer

When successful people hear the word no, they immediately start to think how they can find another way. When a successful person comes across a challenge, instead of wondering 'whether' it can be done, they wonder 'how' it can be done.

Work hard

Successful people value their time and know that their hard work will eventually pay off. They expect extraordinary results from themselves and put in 100%.

Success does not happen overnight. It is a step by step, year by year process that can be frustrating and confusing at times. By around the five year mark you will usually start to see real results.

Unfortunately, most people quit before this happens. That goes some way to explaining why there are only a small percent of successful people. The successful people keep at it until finally they hit their desired target.

Become a lifelong learner

When I read about successful people who started out with nothing, I found that it was often their willingness and determination to learn and change that took them forward.

Successful people constantly ask questions. They know that learning never stops. There are always new ways of looking at things and there is always more to learn. They attend seminars, listen to CDs and read every day. They take action on what they learn, pushing themselves further, and opening the door for more learning.

Believe in yourself

Everybody at some stage in their lives lacks self belief. We all wonder at some point if we have the confidence and skills to get where we want to go. The difference is that the successful people don't allow their self doubts and negative thoughts to consume them. They accept their faults and learn to believe in themselves through retraining their negative thoughts into positive thoughts.

Be self reliant and take responsibility

Successful people do not complain or blame others for the way their life is going. They take responsibility for their own future.

Once they have made a decision, they get into action. They do not wait for anybody's approval to achieve what they desire.

Successful people have a vision and a plan and they take action themselves to make it happen.

Live in the 'now'

Successful people do not waste time; they use each minute to create their vision. They know that now is the only time they have.

When they are at home they focus on their family, when they are at work they focus on work, when they are out for dinner they enjoy their meal. They achieve a lot by working hard in the 'now'. Every day is valuable and they take full advantage of each day.

Visualise the future

Successful people have a vision. They do things others say can't be done.

Their vision is so strong they live their lives as if their vision has already been achieved. Living in this way creates the space for reality to catch up with the vision, and soon they have achieved their goal.

Act fast

Successful people don't waste time thinking about what needs to be done; they just start it and finish it. When they see an opportunity they take immediate action.

They understand that the faster you move the quicker you accomplish your tasks. They never procrastinate and do not get side tracked. They keep focused until the job is complete.

Network

Successful people know the importance of surrounding themselves with other successful people. They attend mastermind groups or entrepreneur clubs to help guide them in their desired direction.

Successful people value friendships and relationships. They are interested in everybody from the waitress to the millionaire and communicate with each person on the same level.

Have commitment and determination

Successful people have such a strong ambition that they have no choice but to achieve what they have set out to achieve. They have the drive, determination and enthusiasm that keeps them focused on their vision.

They have made a commitment for the long haul, knowing their pay off will eventually come. They don't worry about the hard work because they know what will follow.

Make a commitment to focus on one of these areas each day. With practice they will become habits and you will have developed the traits and characteristics of a successful person.

Part Three
WHERE TO NEXT

Make this Book the Beginning of Your Learning Journey

This might be the first book you have read in a while, but that's fine, because many people do not read books at all. The power of reading to learn, and applying the knowledge, cannot be underestimated.

When my counsellor Donna recommended I read a book, the one I chose was The Courage to Heal by Elen Bass & Laura David. It was a guide for women survivors of child sexual abuse. I read it in a week and can't begin to tell you what a difference it made to me. It gave me strength to get through my issues, made me realise what I was experiencing was normal, and most importantly it helped me realise I could do something about my issues.

From then on I was on a mission of self development. The next book I bought was Men Are From Mars, Women Are From Venus by John Gray. After living for seven years in a dysfunctional relationship where I was told my behaviours were wrong, I wanted to understand the difference between males and females. This book helped me to realise that I was normal, as females and males are totally different and should not be expected to have the same reactions and feelings. The book also gave me an insight into the male world and affirmed for me that the relationship I had been in was not the right one for me.

After this I wanted to work on my anger. I had become so accustomed to angry outbursts in my violent relationship that I had learned to use the same angry behaviour as my partner. I didn't want to be angry any more so I bought The Dance Of Anger by Harriet Lerner. This book took me right inside myself to understand why the anger was happening. I came to recognise the cycle of anger and was given the tools to change my anger patterns. Every time I began to feel sweaty I knew I was getting angry. This book helped to transform me into the loving Mum I knew was inside me all those years. I have also been able to help my children learn to understand the difference between healthy and unhealthy anger.

Once I had used the power of books to work on myself, it was now time to work on where I was going in life. I really wanted to live near the beach and run my own business, so the next book I purchased was Feel The Fear And Do It Anyway by Susan Jeffers. Wow, if you have a fear you want to deal with, buy this book. You will not have that fear for much longer! Within a week of reading the book I had resigned from my job and moved to the beach. I just went ahead and did it and am so glad I did.

After that I wanted to learn about successful business women so off I went and purchased The Secrets of Female Entrepreneurs Exposed by Dale Beaumont. Ladies, if you want to build your own business, this is a great book to read. I read with amazement about the obstacles these women faced and how they got over them. I kept thinking 'If they can get over those challenges, what is stopping me?'

I emailed each and every woman whose story appeared in the book and asked them questions. Can you believe seventy percent of those women emailed or phoned me back? This is the power of taking action, not just reading. The advice the ladies gave me was so simple but so helpful. I learnt that being in business does not have to always be hard work. The beginning is hard but once you reach a certain level it can be so much fun.

I then wanted to build up www.SignsBanners.com.au so I bought the book The Emyth Revisited by Michael E. Gerber. This book is great for learning about systems in your business. It explains in easy to understand language why most small businesses don't work and what to do about it.

By then it had become a habit to buy a book whenever I wanted to learn something.

My son was facing anger issues and so I bought I'm Not Bad, I'm Just Mad by Laurence E Shapiro. Each night we would lie in his bed together and work through the activities. I couldn't believe the transformation in my son after we read this book and took action together. Now he says 'Mum I can feel my heart racing, I can feel I am getting angry so I am going to walk away for five minutes'. My son is ten years old. Books are so very powerful.

Of course it's all well and good to read a book, however it's the ACTION you take that counts. You can read until the cows come home but if you don't take action on your learnings, don't be surprised if nothing changes.

As of today, make it a habit to read as many books as you need to. If you are a slow reader, great, read slow, but make sure you take action on the learnings. If you have no money, great, borrow books from the library. If your excuse is that you don't have time, great, make time. Get up an hour earlier and read a chapter each morning, read a chapter in your lunch break, or go to bed an hour earlier to read.

Everything You Desire Will Come to You

Have you heard of the movie and book phenomenon The Secret?

When the movie first came out I had no idea how the universe worked but I totally GOT IT once I saw the movie. So much of the stuff they talked about was actually happening to me.

After years of taking small steps and taking action in the right direction, always believing I would get there, the universe opened up for me and was throwing my desires at me from all angles. When I started to understand how the universe had played its part in transforming my life, I wanted to share what I had learned with others.

I wanted to record the steps I had taken and the lessons I had learned to help others take responsibility for their lives and allow the universe to open up and deliver their desires to them.

What I had learned was that, as soon as you:

- get clear
- accept who you are
- know exactly what you want, and
- are living congruently with your unique values,

the universe will rally around you and things will fall into place.

Once you put these steps in place, all your dreams, visions and desires will come to you. It may seem at first that your dream is so big there is absolutely no way it can be achieved and you don't even know where to begin. Once you start implementing this information though, everything will come to you; it will begin to appear right at just the right time and the right place.

I know this may seem a little 'out there', and perhaps just wishful thinking, so let me give you an example of how this happened in my own life.

Once I had done the same exercises you have done in this book, amazing things started to happen. I had a grand plan to build houses for homeless young Mums and their babies, and then use these exercises to empower them to transform their lives. It seemed like one of those dreams that was too big to ever actually happen.

I rang to enquire about a coaching course to help me on my way but it was $10,000. I quietly said 'thank you I will get back to you' knowing full well this was not going to happen as I did not have $10,000. When the lady followed up my enquiry I told her I would do the course when I had the funds. She offered to sponsor me so that I could complete the course for free.

After the coaching course I went to a webmaster and asked him to build my website. I had the money to pay him to create my website, but he said he wanted to build it for me as what I was doing was close to his heart. He built the whole website for free.

Once I had my website up and running, I began running free workshops for young Mums. It soon occurred to me that this information was so powerful that I could take it further and do motivational speaking. Not long after, the media called me wanting to do a story.

My business was growing so fast I hired a business coach, who put me onto the *Money and You* program. At this program I heard Susan Barton speak. Susan is the founder of The Lighthouse Foundation, who run homes for underprivileged kids. She just happened to be in the process of opening her very first house for homeless young Mums and their babies. I called Susan and asked to jump on board. I am now the Ambassador of the Lighthouse Foundation's Mums 'n Bubs program.

The committee members at the Lighthouse Foundation needed a speaker to promote the Mums 'n Bubs homes. One of the ladies introduced me to the speaker Winston Marsh. He helped me put my keynote speech together, and suddenly I became a motivational speaker just as I had planned.

The media coverage for the Mums 'n Bubs program helped get my name out and people started to hear about the information I wanted to share. A book publisher called me wanting to publish my book.

I started a Facebook page and commented on someone else's post. This comment attracted someone to me who invited me to a business group. At the business group were two very successful speakers. Later I met one of them for coffee, and he gave me some fabulous information about the speaking industry.

This led me to meeting extremely influential people who I used to watch on TV and read about in books. These people became my mentors and now I associate with them all the time.

When I started to write my book, bestselling authors appeared in my life at just the right moment to give me feedback on writing the book. When I needed the front cover graphic designed, the graphic designer I most wanted turned up. He had done branding work for one of my main business mentors. As I was getting ready to go to print, a top Australian copywriter appeared to help me with my selling point.

Every day something happens to take me closer to by BIG dream.

Don't tell me this is all coincidental. This is how the universe works when you open your mind and take note of everything that happens each hour of each day. Every time something happens, there is a message for you if you are listening.

Let me say it again:

As soon as you:

- get clear
- accept who you are
- know exactly what you want, and
- are living congruently with your unique values,

the universe will rally around you and things will fall into place.

Change Your Life, One Step at a Time

If you would love to change your life, live your dreams and achieve your goals, Stacey is offering a coaching program to help kick start your journey.

Grab this incredible opportunity to work up close and personal with Stacey through this amazing program.

Stacey has shown that no matter where we come from, we each have the power to change our lives.

You will be supported step by step as you release old habits and take on the characteristics and traits of highly successful people. Learn how to pinpoint your passion, live according to your values and prepare a plan of action for your new life.

As part of Stacey's commitment to helping change the lives of those around her, every year five lucky young mums aged 14-25 will have the chance to win the course for free. Contact us at www.StaceyCurrie. com if you would like to be considered to be part of this special group.

If you believe you are totally committed to becoming who you always dreamed you could be, and can't wait to get there, contact us now at www.StaceyCurrie.com.

Stacey Speaks

Stacey is in demand as a speaker for corporate and keynote events.

She uses her experiences of triumphing over obstacles to inspire others to reach their own goals and achieve success in their lives.

Speaker Topics Include:

1. Goal setting and action taking
2. Marketing your business without spending a cent
3. Building a million dollar company
4. Commit yourself to success
5. Surround yourself with positive people
6. Work, life balance
7. Believe you are the most amazing person
8. Dealing with fear
9. Discovering your Values
10. Become the person you put on a pedestal

To enquire about inviting Stacey to your event, contact the Stacey Currie team at:

Fax: 03 9775 1606

PO Box 8671

Carrum Downs, Vic 3201

Stacey@StaceyCurrie.com

www.StaceyCurrie.com

Passion Quotes

*P*lease read these quotes slowly so that you can take in their full meaning. I used to read quotes really quickly, and finally realised I wasn't taking in their meaning. Now I re-read quotes until I have a clear understanding of the meaning.

A great leader's courage to fulfil his vision comes from passion, not position.

- John Maxwell

Above all, be true to yourself, and if you cannot put your heart in it, take yourself out of it.

- Author unknown

Develop a passion for learning. If you do, you will never cease to grow.

- Anthony J. D 'Angelo

Don't ask yourself what the world needs; ask yourself what makes you come alive. And then go and do that. Because what the world needs are people who have come alive.

- Harold Whitman

Follow your passion, and success will follow you.

- Arthur Buddhold

If you have ever felt such tremendous enthusiasm and desire for something that you would gladly spend all your waking hours working on it, that you would happily do without pay, then you have found your passion.

- Sharon Cook & Graciela Sholander

Try to pursue the very things that you are passionate about. That is the difference between good and great!

- Shawn Doyle

The more intensely we feel about an idea or a goal, the more assuredly the idea, buried deep in our subconscious, will direct us along the path to its fulfilment.

- Earl Nightingale

We all need to look into the dark side of our nature- that's where the energy is, the passion. People are afraid of that because it holds pieces of us we're busy denying.

- Sue Grafton

Without passion you don't have energy, without energy you have nothing.

- Donald Trump

Lighthouse Foundation

We all crave success in our lives – and success can be gained so easily! For us to achieve this success, the key is to give back! It is very important to understand that by giving back to the community we can not only make a difference in other people's lives, but it helps to change our lives for the better as well.

I am privileged to be an Ambassador for the Lighthouse Foundation – a fantastic organisation that aims to end the growing problem of youth homelessness in Australia. Over the past 20 years, Lighthouse has been achieving its vision by providing long-term safe, secure accommodation in a family-style setting for Australia's most vulnerable and traumatised kids. Combined with this loving home environment, Lighthouse works with each young person individually, enabling them to access a range of tailored and intensive supports, one to one therapeutic counselling and education programs so that they can be healed and rebuild their lives, develop the confidence and skills they need and, when they are ready, move out into interdependent living and eventually become contributing members of the community.

Where do I come in? My special interest is in helping the homeless young Mums and their babies. Each of them has suffered a long-term history of abuse and neglect. I know, from personal experience, that without the Lighthouse homes and support programs, these young Mums and their babies could quite easily end up living in violent relationships or on the streets without any support. Our young women deserve better!

www.staceycurrie.com

The distinctive quality of the Lighthouse 'Mums 'n Bubs' program is the whole-of-life approach. Beyond the safe, long-term accommodation at Lighthouse, the facilities and support that are offered foster the development of the most loving, nurturing, together, Mums... something every baby deserves – and something most of these young women never experienced themselves when they were growing up. By modelling a loving environment, the young mothers learn how to raise their baby – with love and nurture – so that both Mum and baby continue to thrive and grow, and ultimately reach their full potential.

And when they are ready the young mothers at Lighthouse are encouraged to finish school or complete a TAFE course so that they can truly be independent, gain employment and be personally fulfilled.

I am committed to supporting the 'Mums 'n Bubs' program. My goal is to support the Lighthouse Foundation in delivering new programs to the 'Mums 'n Bubs' and to support Lighthouse in continuous growth to provide the model of care throughout Australia. With your help and support, young Mums will be given more opportunities while living in a safe environment with their babies. This will break the cycle of youth homelessness - not only for these young women, but for the next generation as well.

Remember - you can help make a difference in the lives of many young Mums and their babies – and achieve your own success at the same time. So jump on board and help me kick my goal.

How, you ask?

Easy

Call the Lighthouse Foundation to make a donation on 03 9093 7500 or go to the website www.LighthouseFoundation.org.au

Resources to Share

These books helped me get through various obstacles and I hope they can help you too.

Self Development Books:

The Courage To Heal- Elen Bass & Laura David

The Dance of Anger- Harriet Lerner

Feel The Fear And Do It Anyway- Susan Jeffers

I'm Not Bad, I'm Just Mad- Lawrence E, Shapiro, Zach Pelter- Heller, Anna F. Greenwald

Business Books:

The Emyth Revisited- Michael E. Gerber

How to be Wildy Wealthy Fast- Sandy Forster

Rich Dad Poor Dad- Robert Kiyosaki

The Secret- Rhonda Byrne

You Were Born Rich- Bob Proctor

The Gratitude Effect- Dr John Demartini

The Riches Within- Dr John Demartini

Eat That Frog- Brian Tracy

Anything by Brad Sugars

Anything by Jeff Gitomer

Anything by Seth Godin

Female Entrepreneurs Exposed- Dale Beaumont

The Science Of Success- Wallace D. Wattles

The One Minute Millionaire- Mark Victor Hansen

Think and Grow Rich- Napoleon Hill

Celebrity Branding You- Nick Nanton & J.W. Dicks